SELF-

HELPLESS

The Greatest Self-Help Books
You'll Never Read

SELF-HELPLESS

The Greatest Self-Help Books You'll Never Read

By
Jonathan Bines
and
Gary Greenberg

Designed by Jeanne Hayden

CAREER PRESS

Franklin Lakes, NJ

SELF-HELPLESS
Designed by Jeanne Hayden
Printed in the U.S.A. by Book-mart Press

To order this title, please call toll-free 1-800-CAREER-1 (NJ and Canada: 201-848-0310) to order using VISA or MasterCard, or for further information on books from Career Press.

The Career Press, Inc., 3 Tice Road, PO Box 687
Franklin Lakes, NJ 07417

Library of Congress Cataloging-in-Publication Data

Bines, Jonathan.
  Self-helpless : the greatest self-help books you'll never read /
by Jonathan Bines and Gary Greenberg.
    p. cm.
  ISBN 1-56414-411-9
  1. Success—Humor. 2. Self-help techniques—Humor.
I. Greenberg, Gary, 1964-   II. Title.
PN6231.S83856   1999
818' 5402—dc21
                                                  99-11636
                                                      CIP

> *To our parents, who believed in us even when trained professionals told them not to.*

Acknowledgements

We'd like to acknowledge all of the people without whose time, patience, and generosity this book would not have been possible, except for those who have expressly requested that we not. First and foremost, our graphic designer and chief illustrator, Jeanne Hayden, without whose creativity and hard work this book would not have been possible. We're also deeply indebted to the illustrious crew at Career Press: Mike Gaffney, Stacey A. Farkas, Jackie Michaels, and in particular Ron Fry and Anne Brooks, for their inexhaustible enthusiasm for the project and tireless work on its behalf. Thanks also to our other illustrators: Chris Kalb, Jessica Miller, Kristina Zugar, Pete Wood, the brothers Henning, and Christoph Alberti, and photographers Mimi Schultz, Amy Elliott, and Neil Greenberg. We're grateful to those who agreed, against their better judgement, to appear in the book: Marlene, Neil, and Marcy Greenberg, Jon Feinberg, Lynn Harris, Marietta Danil, Amy E. Betelho, Dierdre Sullivan, Cynthia Becht, Johnathan McClain, Sean Hagerty, Mike Kasper, Louie Vitiello, and Susanne Bines. Thanks to Chris Mazzilli and the Gotham Comedy Club, and to Modern Sofa for offering locations for photo shoots, and to Barnes & Noble Astor Place (where we wrote the thing). Many others provided support and assistance along the way: Thanks to the whole Bines and Greenberg clans and to all our friends. And special thanks to Margot Weiss, Jeremy Kareken, Herb Emanuelson, Dan Handalian, Mike Liss, Jennifer Lang, and of course Alexandra and Jeanne, the inspiration for all this lunacy.

Introduction

Looking back on our amazing journey of personal growth, it's hard to believe that just a few short years ago, we knew nothing about the self-help industry, its major authors, and seminal texts. Unfamiliar with even the masterworks of the genre—*The Road Less Traveled; The Power of Positive Thinking; I'm OK, You're OK*—we went about our unexamined lives, hopelessly out of touch with our inner children, our recovering artists, our personal power, our wild men, our secret gardens, our guardian angels, our T-Factors, our past lives, our planetary origins, and our final exits.

All that changed one crisp, fall day in April, 1995, when, climbing in the Himalayas, we were caught in a blinding snowstorm and forced to take refuge in a nearby cave. As our eyes became adjusted to the light, we discovered a grim scene: a lone mountaineer, frozen in repose, his lifeless fingers clutching a weather-beaten copy of Steven Covey's *7 Habits of Highly Effective People*. To pass the time until the storm cleared, we extracted the book from his icy grip and started reading. By the time we left that cave three days later, our lives had changed forever.

Since then, we've devoted our lives to self-improvement. With every book we read, we discover new dysfunctions to remedy, new inadequacies to correct, new addictions from which to recover. Our voracious appetite for the genre has taken us far beyond the best-sellers, into the world of the self-help also-rans, the books that never made it off the shelves. These forgotten gems, overlooked by a fickle reading public, languish, spines unbent, in remainder bins and authors' basements. It is our profound hope that, in perusing the dust-jacket reproductions anthologized herein, you may stumble across that one special work that has the power to transform your life as ours have been transformed.

Peace.
J.B. and G.G.
December 1, 1998

Disclaimer
and
Notice of Limitation of Liability

This book [hereinafter referred to as "the book"] is intended solely for the private use of the reader ["the reader"]. Neither the book, nor any portion thereof, nor any portion of any portion thereof (ad infinitum) may for any reason be reproduced, revised, annotated, deconstructed, corrected for spelling, folded into an origami frog, or read aloud with a humorous foreign accent without the express written consent of the authors and the publisher.

The authors ["the authors"] do hereby deny, refute, reject, quitclaim, and hold unaccountable themselves and all parties even vaguely related to themselves for any adverse reactions that any second, third, or other whole-numbered party may have to the book, including but not limited to boredom, headache, nausea, frustration, or fatigue; and do further deny, refute, dismiss, reject, and insult the mother of any and all claimants, individually or formed into discussion groups, who may now or in the future seek compensation in the form of money, gift certificates, sexual favors, non-medically indicated cosmetic surgery, or any other form of restitution for any and all injuries that may result from the book or the reading or transport thereof, including but not limited to paper cuts, trauma from smacking of palm against forehead in dismay, or eye injuries from repeated rolling.

The reader hereby explicitly acknowledges that the book is a work of parody and that to initiate legal action against the authors or publisher of a work of parody would be, and is acknowledged to be, lame. Consequently, the reader hereby agrees to forego any legal remedy he or she may have against the author or publisher for libel, defamation, or trademark infringement, and instead to submit any such claims to binding arbitration before a panel of independent adjudicators to be selected by the authors and comprised of the authors' friends from the New York City stand-up comedy circuit.

By reading this sentence, the reader indicates his or her agreement to the terms set forth herein.

THE POWWOW
OF
POSITIVE
THINKING

Living Life Without Reservations!

Werner Bear Heart

DON'T ASK "WHY"– ASK "HOW!"

"*How* can I love my life?" "*How* can I improve my relationships?" "*How* can I achieve my dreams?" You'll find out how, when you join Indian Chief-Turned-Motivational-Speaker Werner ("Bucky") Bear Heart at his revolutionary seminar of transformation and personal growth, *The Powwow of Positive Thinking!*

The Powwow combines the ancient wisdom of the Cherokees with the modern motivational techniques of the EST movement. Over the course of an intensive five-day retreat, participants undergo a grueling regimen alternating between traditional ceremonial rituals and humiliating verbal abuse designed to break down their soulless Western belief structure and reconstruct them as Native American Spiritual Warriors.

Thousands have already taken The Powwow. Here's what some of them have to say:

"I was a marketing manager for a major corporation, but I wasn't sure what I wanted to do with my life. Then, in an airport lobby, someone handed me a pamphlet about Chief Bucky. After taking his Powwow, I finally realized my true calling: To hang around in airport lobbies and hand out pamphlets about Chief Bucky!"

\- John Proud Frond

"I had a lot of doubts before I took The Powwow. Now I don't have any more doubts."

-Vanessa Broken Nostril Feather

"I encourage everyone to experience The Powwow and see for themselves. Whether they then choose to sell all their possessions and donate the proceeds to the Chief Bucky World Transformation Development Fund, as I did, is their own personal decision."

\- Bill Limping Beaver

1099 182 3746

$9.95

THE
STARR
HITE
REPORT
ON
PRESIDENTIAL
SEXUALITY

"What the President does behind closed doors, in the privacy of his own home, is very interesting!"
—BOB WOODWARD, author of *ALL THE PRESIDENT'S WOMEN*

KENNETH STARR AND SHERE HITE

"Penetrating!" –*CIGAR AFICIONADO*

Unimpeachable Research...

William Jefferson Clinton is the President of the United States, Commander in Chief of the armed forces, and the acknowledged leader of the free world. Yet, until now, we have had no insight into the masturbatory habits, erotic fantasies, or consensual sexual activities of the nation's highest elected official.

In *The Starr/Hite Report*, famed sexologist Shere Hite teams up with smut-mongering independent prosecutor Kenneth Starr to produce the most comprehensive survey ever conducted of the sexual proclivities and peccadilloes of a sitting president. Applying probing sociological analysis and coercive prosecutorial tactics, Starr and Hite leave no Tripp untapped, no stain unswabbed in their efforts to expose the activities of the little Head of State that lurks below the beltway.

INCLUDES *Alphabetized Bimbography!*

"I thought I was some kind of freak, but this book really put my mind at ease."
                    –*GERALD FORD*

$10.95

298765 20986

THE
BOOK OF
RHETORICAL
QUESTIONS

BY Y. MEE, PH.D.

"Is this a great book? Do I love this book?"
— Sid Greenfield, United Creative Artists, Hollywood

Who couldn't benefit from this book?

MOTHERS	What have I done to deserve this?
FATHERS	Do you want to send me to an early grave?
MAFIOSI	What are you, some kind of a smart guy?
HIGH SCHOOL PRINCIPALS	What do I have to do to get through to you?
HIGHWAY PATROLMEN	Where's the fire?
HUNTERS	Does a bear shit in the woods?
BARDS	To be or not to be?
HOMIES	What's up with that?
STAND-UP COMEDIANS	What's the deal with airplane food?
MOVIE VILLAINS	Do you have any idea who you're dealing with?
FRIENDS OF CRAZY DRIVERS	Do you want to get us all killed?
FEMALE BAR PATRONS	What's a girl got to do to get a drink around here?
ELDERLY JEWISH MEN	Nu?

So now that you know how great it is, why not pick up your own copy today?

$10.95

"What's the secret to great ventriloquism? My lips are sealed!"
- Master Vent Captain Pete

25 MILLION
Dummies can't be wrong

VENTRILOQUISM FOR DUMMIES™

A Reference for the Rest of Us, and Our Little Friends

Your Puppetmaster Guide To Shameless Self-Promotion™

Tight-Lipped Tactics For Keeping a "Quiet Mouth"™

The Hands-In Approach To Finding Your Dream Dummy™

BONUS

"Buy this book and I'll be your right-hand man"

Does ventriloquism make your palms sweat? When you do the drinking trick, does water come out of your nose? Are you sick and tired of bookers and agents pulling _your_ strings? Well, pack up your puppet and come with us!

CODE RED™

Shows you time-tested cover-ups for onstage disasters

LIP READERS™

THROW YOUR VOICE
PUPPET TIME
STAGE FRIGHT

Points out a host of related reference materials

TIME OUT™

Presents tips for maintaining your sanity

INCLUDES CLASSIC ROUTINES FOR EVERY SITUATION

Clean
VENT: You're silly.
DUMMY: No, you're silly.
VENT: I'm silly?
DUMMY: You're the one talking to a piece of wood.

Naughty
DUMMY: You know why chicks dig me?
VENT: No, (Dummy's Name), why do chicks dig you?
DUMMY: Because I've got a wood pecker.
VENT: Stop it!

Disgusting
VENT: You're looking a bit stiff today, (Dummy's Name).
DUMMY: That's because you've got your arm shoved halfway up my ass.
VENT: You're incorrigible!

About the authors:
Howie Allen, the 1996 Edgar Bergen Award winner, has been a professional vent for 23 years, and spent a decade on tour with his one-man, one-puppet interpretation of _Waiting For Godot_.

Mortimer Snell was carved from a single block of old growth Tuscaloosa pine.

"Sock Making Sense!™ A No-Holes-Darned Look At Shari Lewis and Lambchop ⓤ"

$12.98

Embraced
by the Lite FM

The Remarkable Near-Death Easy-Listening
Experience of Betty Early

"Betty has heard the angels
singing, and they're singing
<u>Mandy</u> by Barry Manilow."

– Dr. Bernie Gross, author of
<u>I Write the Prescriptions</u>

Against All Odds...

On November 13, 1993, during routine oral surgery, 31-year-old wife and mother Betty Early received an overdose of anesthesia, and her heart stopped beating. It didn't start again for 17 minutes. In the most vivid account of a near-death experience ever published, Mrs. Early relays the powerful message of love and music she received from beyond – and tells how you can get the message, simply by opening your heart and tuning into the Lite FM.

On the Son of God:

"There was Jesus, doing karaoke. He was singing *Muskrat Love*. Somehow, it all made sense..."

On God's Message to Humanity:

"He said, 'Just tell them: I'm on top of the world looking down on creation, so cherish the love you have, and don't stop believing.'"

On the Joyous Afterlife:

"We're going to party, karamu, fiesta, forever!"

• • •

"Read it to me one more time! Once is never enough for a book like this!"
– Tenille

"IIIIIIIIIIIYYYYYIIIIIIIIIIIIIIIIIIIYYYYIIIIIIIIII...enjoyed it."
– Whitney Houston

"Heaven grooves to the smooth sounds of soft, relaxing Lite FM, 24-hours a day, eternally commercial-free."
– Pope John Paul II

About the Author: Betty Early is once, twice, three times a lady, a daydream believer, and a Caribbean queen. She's had joy, she's had fun, she's had seasons in the sun, and likes leather and lace, piña coladas, and getting caught in the rain. A summer breeze makes her feel fine. She currently resides between the moon and New York City with her poetry man, her part-time lover, and a dog named Boo.

$16.95

32887227 233 386

Thomas A. Smith, M.D.

author of STAYING OJ

I'M OJ –
YOU'RE OJ

The Transgressional Analysis
Breakthrough That Will Leave
You Feeling "100% NOT GUILTY"

Transgressional Analysis...
Because You're Only As Guilty As You Feel

We've all done things in life we're not proud of. Some have cheated on their income taxes; others have betrayed a friend's trust. Some of us may even have slaughtered our wife and her friend in cold blood near the front gate of her Brentwood condominium. Whatever our particular "transgression," we all know the unpleasant feeling associated with acts of premeditated wrongdoing: GUILT.

Now, there is an alternative. In *I'm OJ, You're OJ*, Dr. Thomas Smith, the inventor of Transgressional Analysis (TA), shows you how to eliminate guilt feelings and live life to the fullest — no matter how heinous your misdeeds. With Smith's guidance, you'll learn how to take advantage of the same techniques that helped the Juice to transform himself from the unmistakably guilty-looking fugitive in the white Bronco into the self-confident and adamantly innocent golfer and author of *I Want To Tell You*.

Whether you've taken a human life or just an extra slice of pecan pie, *I'm OJ, You're OJ* can show you how to remove unwanted remorse painlessly and permanently and start living a 100% NOT GUILTY life!

"Yes, I read it...and I'd read it again!"
– G. GORDON LIDDY

WHAT IS TRANSGRESSIONAL ANALYSIS?

Transgressional Analysis (TA) takes a multidisciplinary approach to guilt elimination, drawing upon biological determinism to show that you had to do it, Objectivism to show you were justified in doing it, Eastern philosophy to show there's no "you" to have done it, critical legal studies to show there's no guilt or innocence, contemporary literary theory to show that there's no true or false, moral relativism to show there's no right or wrong, and existentialism to point out that, in any case, there's no point feeling guilty about it since you're destined to die a meaningless death in a cold and indifferent universe.

THE HABITS OF 7
HIGHLY
DEFECTIVE
PEOPLE

Leadership Secrets of Mutants
From the Editors of *Modern Deformity*

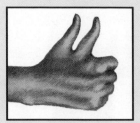

"Two Thumbs Up!"
– *MUTANT BUSINESS QUARTERLY*

I n this one-of-a-kind book, seven of America's leading corporate mutants reveal the secrets that have taken them to the top. You'll find tips on downsizing from Larry Mink, ALCOA's eight-inch-tall Vice President of Process Re-Engineering; hardball negotiating tactics from Freddie "Hammer Head" Fazzioli of Allied Waste Disposal; and advice on improving group dynamics from seven-headed Hydra-man Alan Riding, who comprises the entire board of directors of the John Deere Corporation.

Having trouble breaking through that glass ceiling? Find out what worked for Norelco Marketing VP Sheila Moskowitz (a.k.a. The 90-Foot Woman). Think you've got a "nose for business"? Well, Walter Mitchell has twelve of them! And this savvy Smith Barney broker will show you how to sniff out investment opportunities that others may have missed. You'll also read an in-depth interview with Marion and Ed Little, the Hunchbacks of Northern Telecom, two of the leading proponents of Total Quasimodo Management (TQM).

"This book is an invaluable tool for any manager seeking to improve his...his...oh, no, not again! AAAH! GRRRR! RAAAARGH! HRRRRRAIGH!"
– MELVIN "WOLFMAN" PHELPS, AUTHOR OF *CORPORATE ACCOUNTING THE WOLFMAN WAY*

U.S. $14.00
Can $18.00

78055 805746

Martha Stewart

Loving

Perfect Sex!

It's a good thing...

*S*he helped you plan the perfect wedding – now let her help you consummate it! In this handsome volume, Martha Stewart shows you how to transform a humdrum sex life into a smorgasbord of erotic possibility using everyday household items and fresh, seasonal ingredients. Guided by Martha's helpful illustrations and instructions "any idiot could follow," you'll soon be molding and casting festive chocolate sexual aids, candy-coating and monogramming your birth control pills, and whittling a phallic latticework of your own design onto a swishy birch rod.

Quilted Penis Cozy

12-Grain Erotic Muffins

You'll get recipes for delicious, low-fat edible undergarments, Martha's "Quickie" Blender Spanish Fly (fennel is the secret ingredient!) and a selection of sweet and savory hypo-allergenic genital toppings. Home video buffs will appreciate Martha's tips on proper lighting, pacing, and mise-en-scène. And in the chapter on entertaining,

Yuletide Holly Cuffs

you'll find detailed instructions for planning an intimate menage-à-trois, a neighborhood wife-swapping party – even a full-blown Roman orgy! Now *that's* living!

Martha's Saucy Secrets:

"No sexual encounter is complete without a hand-dipped post-coital mint..."

"For sensitivity and tensile strength, nothing beats a good old fashioned hand-knotted condom made of fresh lamb entrails..."

"If your sexual partners spend time on their hands and knees – as mine do – you'll find that strategically-placed, hand-woven Bhutanese runners can prevent chafing while reducing wear-and-tear on the carpeting."

...A really gooooood thing!

The Courage to Squeal

A Prudent Wiseguy's Guide to Ratting Out The Mob

By Sammy "The Weasel" Formaggio

Bestselling Author Of

Codefendant No More

More than 100,000 Sold Down The River!

Look Who's Talking
...And Walking!

If you're ready to end your unhealthy relationship with the Cosa Nostra, Sammy "The Weasel" Formaggio is here to help. A notorious stool pigeon, government informant, and author of eight tell-all bestsellers including *What to Expect When You're Defecting* and *Double-Crossing Delancey*, Formaggio has won a reputation among G-Men and button men alike as "the finking man's Dale Carnegie."

In *The Courage To Squeal*, Formaggio talks candidly about his own painful experiences trapped in a destructive Family environment. In later chapters, he examines case studies of successful and unsuccessful snitches, and identifies the barriers that keep Mafia members from achieving open, honest communication with federal agents, including guilt feelings, self-esteem issues, and fear of being tossed in a cement mixer and paved into the New York State Thruway.

Hoodlums Rave!

"After I ratted out Big Louie and The Paisano, I felt pretty awful about myself. Your book helped me to remember that, deep down, I'm still a Goodfella."
    – ALPHONSE "TWO-TIME"
        MARSCAPONE

"Thanks to Formaggio, I'm one squeaky wheel who didn't get greased."
    – SALVATORE "SNITCH" PESCATORE

The author and his dog, Brutus.

298765 20986

THE
STELLA STEIN
PROPHECY

Words from the Wise

Estelle R. Stein

*"Mrs. Stein has seen the future and –
between you and me – she worries."*

LEAH HIMMELFARB-ROTH,
AUTHOR OF THE PORTABLE NUDGE

Don't Say She Didn't Warn You...

Stella Stein of Sheepshead Bay, Brooklyn, first realized her remarkable psychic power after the tragic death of her first husband, Mort. "I kept telling him: 'Don't eat the fatty foods! They'll put you in your grave!' And it came to pass exactly as I had foretold."

Science has no explanation for Mrs. Stein's gift of prophecy. Yet since that first supernatural occurrence, Mrs. Stein, the self-proclaimed "Nostradamus of Nostrand Ave." has experienced hundreds of similar psychic episodes. Consider these astounding examples:

- On March 2, 1987, Vernon Kopf, a neighbor, mentioned to Stella that he was heading to the boardwalk for a plate of fried clams. As he was departing, Stella shouted to him, "For God's sake, chew them well, you shouldn't choke to death!" Mr. Kopf is alive today.

- On February 28, 1991, Dan Bostwell was purchasing a lottery ticket at the corner store when Stella intervened: "Don't waste your money on those things! You'll never win!" Dan bought the ticket anyway, and lost his dollar.

- On June 15, 1993, Stella was in the car running errands with her son, Howard. "Keep driving like a maniac," she warned, "and you're going to get us into an accident!" Howard turned to argue, and plowed into a parked car.

Now, in *The Stella Stein Prophecy*, Mrs. Stein uses the same amazing psychic abilities to predict what may lie in store for you if you don't clean your plate, sit far enough away from the TV, or check for ticks after playing in the tall grass. So if you know what's good for you, you'll read this book from cover to cover. Only make sure there's good light – you don't want to ruin your eyes.

$10.50

485 3746 273

WHAT COLOR IS YOUR PARASITE?

The Complete Parasite Pet Guide

Get in touch with your inner worm!

Richard Giardia

BE THE PERFECT HOST!

Tippy Tapeworm   **Manny Mealworm**

They say that when you've found the right pet, you can feel it in your gut – and nobody knows that better than Richard Giardia! A successful breeder of prize-winning tapeworms, roundworms, and hookworms, he has introduced thousands of people to the unique joys that come from owning and caring for that special someone who's "infestin' your intestine!"

Benefits of Ownership:

- WEIGHT LOSS – You'll shed pounds and keep them off when you're "eating for two."

- HEALTH – Scientists have proven that caring for a pet can actually lower blood pressure – and a blood-sucking buddy can be twice as effective!

- CLEANLINESS – You never have to worry about walking your parasite or changing litter. "Slinky" is as potty-trained as you are!

What Color Is Your Parasite? gives you everything you'll need to successfully select, ingest, and care for your little live-in guest. The book offers complete health care and nutrition information, plus advice on spaying and neutering, and correcting problem behavior in your worm. You'll read about ten simple tricks you can teach your worm – including "Fetch The Jujubee" and "Nostril Peek-A-Boo" – guaranteed to leave your friends and family doubled over!

Fanny Flatworm   **Molly Ringworm**

$16.00

*"Why did the chicken cross the
road? To help thousands of people
sort out their emotional difficulties."*
– M. Scott Peck

Chicken Suit
for the Soul

A NEW THERAPY
Benjamin Crisp M.D., Ph.D.

People Are Squawking!

You've seen him on *Oprah*, *Geraldo*, and most recently *Good Morning America*, where he gave Regis some of his patented "Free Range Therapy." He's Dr. Benjamin Crisp, the self-proclaimed "Fine Feathered Freud," and the man who's been ruffling feathers throughout the world of psychoanalysis with his bold new methodology.

> *"As a gigantic orange chicken, I'm able to connect with my patients in a way that the old Dr. Crisp never could. They consider me a mother hen, teaching them to spread their wings and fly. And in my nest, there is no such thing as a bad egg."*

Now the good doctor has collected his favorite mcnuggets of wisdom, drawn from his many years as a therapist. *Chicken Suit for the Soul* is the delightful result.

"Hope is the thing with feathers!"
— **Norton Anthology of Poultry**

$12.95

78055

78055 805746

Published by
Bantam Books

The Disenchanted Broccoli Forest

A Twelve-Step Program For Recovering Vegetarians

Abe Akenberger, M.D., Ph.D.
author of: *The Moosemeat Cookbook*
and *Do I Have to Give Up Meat to Be Loved By You?*

"Hello. My name is Tim Whipple, I'm 42 years old, and I am a Vegetarian..."

Tim's is a familiar tale. A biology professor at a well-known liberal arts college, he once enjoyed vegetables in moderation. Then one day at a department function he shared a bag of low-fat granola with a pretty co-ed, and before long, he was spiraling into uncontrolled Vegetarianism. He began hanging around the student housing cooperative, consuming twelve-grain bread and extolling the virtues of composting. He stopped shaving, liberated his lab rats, voted for Ralph Nader. Friends tried to intervene, but felt powerless in the face of his increasing zealotry and culinary isolation.

Fortunately for Tim and others like him, there is hope. In this timely volume, Dr. Abe Akenberger reveals the amazing twelve-step process that has helped his clients overcome their debilitating meat anxieties and regain a healthy relationship with their carnivorousness.

From The Introduction:
"For many of my patients, meat dysfunction can be traced directly back to early childhood trauma. I recall one patient of mine, a bearded and Birkenstocked young vegetarian, who confessed to disturbing, graphic fantasies involving a large, laughing woman force-feeding him thousands of uncooked Ball Park franks. In therapy, we revisited painful scenes from his childhood responsible for his later rejection of meat, such as the constant pressure to win membership to the "Clean Plate Club," and subsequent anxiety when he could not finish. This came out most poignantly in one session during which he achieved a sort of epiphany, shouting, "It wasn't the pot roast, it was my mother!"

$16.95

23451 789011

DO
WHAT
YOU
LOVE,
THE
MONEY
WILL
FOLLOW

*Pursuing
a Career in
Sperm Bank
Donation*

"The key to a pleasurable
and profitable future
is at your fingertips!"
– SELF-ENTERTAINMENT WEEKLY

Phil D. Kupp

What Your Guidance Counselor Never Told You...

It's something you love to do, and you've been practicing every day since you first learned how. But do you have what it takes to make it as a pro? In this gripping book, America's top-grossing sperm donor offers advice you can take to the bank!

ON GETTING STARTED:
"There's a million guys trying to make it in this business, and they all think they've got terrific material. But the opportunities don't create themselves. I sent samples to twenty different agencies before I found one that would even look at my stuff."

ON GETTING THE "BIG BREAK":
"I got my first paying gig as kind of a fluke. I was hanging around the bank, and one of the regulars got poison ivy and couldn't perform, so they asked me to fill in. But there are other ways. A lot of guys start out as production assistants, and go on from there."

ON WORKING OUTSIDE THE SYSTEM:
"If you can't get in with one of the major agencies, you can try to make it as an independent. I know one fellow who started out going door-to-door with an Igloo cooler. Nowadays, you can also meet potential clients on an Internet fertility chat group. And overseas the American gene pool is still considered a status symbol..."

ON THE PRESSURES OF THE JOB:
"It's especially hard when you're trying to juggle work with a relationship. There you'll be, at an intimate moment, whispering those five little words: 'I gave at the office.'"

ON A JOB WELL DONE:
"You see the results of your work, and it's really satisfying. When I pass a new mom on the street, I think, 'Hey – that could be one of mine.'"

276 837 22767

THE
ROAD LES
TRAVELED

A Wacky Road Trip of Self-Discovery

Ride along with Les Noodleman in his 1974 Dodge Dart as he takes to the open road along Route 1-9 in Weehawken, NJ, in search of beef jerky, duct tape, and self-discovery! *The Road Les Traveled* takes you, mile by mile, through his amazing journey.

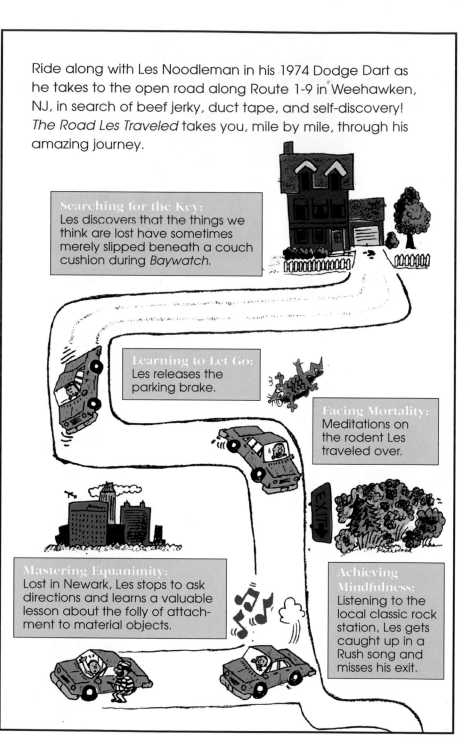

Searching for the Key:
Les discovers that the things we think are lost have sometimes merely slipped beneath a couch cushion during *Baywatch*.

Learning to Let Go:
Les releases the parking brake.

Facing Mortality:
Meditations on the rodent Les traveled over.

Mastering Equanimity:
Lost in Newark, Les stops to ask directions and learns a valuable lesson about the folly of attachment to material objects.

Achieving Mindfulness:
Listening to the local classic rock station, Les gets caught up in a Rush song and misses his exit.

Women Who Run With the Salmon

New Sports for Feminist Environmentalists

"A revolution in
women's athletics!"
TRACK & FIELD & STREAM

A publication of

ESPCA THE SPORTS AND ANIMAL WELFARE NETWORK

$12.95

Springtime in Alaska, and – as

every spring – the icy rivers swarm with salmon headed upstream to spawn. Joining them on their epic journey north is naturalist and endurance swimmer Ella Scharf, world champion in the 10K and 20K Freestyle Upstream Migration.

Scharf is in the vanguard of a new breed of female athlete who take inspiration for their sports from the competition of animals in the wild. In this volume, you'll read her story and those of other remarkable women like her including Karen Ellison, who burrows with the badgers; Babs Nudgeworth, who stampedes with the bison; and Monica Salz, who butted heads with the bull moose until her untimely demise in 1992.

Q&A *WITH ELLA SCHARF*

Why do you run with the salmon?
For me, the sport is all about respect: Respect for the fish, respect for nature, and – ultimately – respect for yourself.

What is your favorite Tour event?
Definitely the Pacific Sprints, because the salmon there are just so inspiring. Atlantic salmon are strong and graceful, and Sockeyes are the most determined, but for sheer, adrenaline-pumping, explosive power, there's nothing to compare to a Chinook.

What do you love most about your sport?
Making it to the finish line. After dodging rocks and debris for hours, to suddenly break through and hit those spawning grounds – what a rush!

"A terrific fitness alternative for women bored with the health club routine!"
– BARBARA WALKER, AUTHOR OF
WOMEN WHO RUN ON THE TREADMILL

298765 20986

Hank Nicholson was only a few classes into his Intermediate Golf seminar when he noticed that something was wrong. Despite the long hours of practice and the latest training gadgets, he simply was not improving. Frustrated and confused, he consulted the course pro, who confirmed his worst fears: At age 27 – with a handicap of 34, a vicious hook off the tee, and the putting skills of a recovering heroin addict – Hank had reached the limits of his golfing abilities.

In this fascinating book, Oliver Sacks, official psychotherapist of the PGA tour and author of seven previous books on golf dysfunction including *The Man Who Mistook His Nine Iron For A Pitching Wedge* and *Why Johnny Can't Putt*, explores the painful and perplexing problem of golf's hopeless cases.

Drawing on more than a decade of experience working with the severely handicapped (25 or greater on the official USGA scale), Sacks offers sensitive portrayals of courageous golfers struggling to cope with a wide range of link-related maladies, from Duffer's Palsy to divoticulitis to chronic iron deficiencies. Whether his patients are struggling from the tee ("I Can't Drive 55!"), on the approach ("Good-bye, Mr. Chip"), or on the green ("Slip Sliding Away"), Sacks puts you right there with them, sharing their joy and frustration as they hack their way to a healthier, more realistic outlook on their games.

ARE YOU A DYSFUNCTIONAL GOLFER?

If you've uttered any of these "red flag" excuses on the course, you may want to seek professional help:

"That's the last time I play Titleists."
"Damn my optician!"
"My woods don't take to this humidity."
"Actually, I was shooting for the other trap."
"I think my caddie is a jinx."
"I would have made it up on the back nine if I hadn't run out of balls."

"If Sacks had been around in my day,
I might still have some hair left!"

— BOB HOPE

ABUNDANT ABUNDANCE

$$\approx$$

A DAYBOOK
of
SACCHARINE
and MILKTOAST

$$\approx$$

Sarah Ban Breathmint
Author of Simple Simplicity

Change into your Snoopy slippers. Warm up some milk. Slide into your big, overstuffed chair and open up ABUNDANT ABUNDANCE, a book of 366 cozy little stories, quotes and activities perfect for temperate souls like yourself. These wonderfully inoffensive entries, one for every day of the year (plus a special one for you!), were designed to give you a permanent case of the warm fuzzies. And if marshmallow fluff starts coming out of your ears, don't worry, that's how the book works!

Reading the entries is only half the fun. You can cut them out, put them on your refrigerator, embroider them onto a pillow, send them to Ann Landers, recite them aloud to strangers on long bus trips, and whisper them to your cats. Doesn't that sound nice?

Create a comfort chest filled with all the things that make you comfy, like soft fabrics, sachets, letters from friends, favorite recipes, dried flowers, doilies, bits of lace, stuffed animals. Take an hour out of each day to lie down inside the chest and have a good cry.

I say YES to the world. YES, people, YES, places, YES, things. YES, animals, YES, minerals, YES, vegetables.

Decorate your cubicle at work in a seasonal fashion. Hang Indian corn and gourds around your computer, and turn your monitor into a jack-o-lantern. Scatter some dried leaves on the floor, and put out a bowl of candy corn.

Think Plenty! Get a big barrel and fill it with beans.

It's better to be a doer who didn't than a don'ter who did! Or vice versa!

$13.95

Life's Little Insurrection Book: The Guerrilla Megillah! Recently declassified by the CIA, this handsome hardbound volume is packed with tips and quips on all aspects of violent resistance: "Sticks and stones may break their bones, so aim for the extremities," etc. Considered a classic of the genre.

Order #28-04902 $37.95

Life's Little Deconstruction Book: Entertaining and enlightening *bon mots* from your favorite French literary theorists, including Derrida, Lacan, and Foucault. Includes old chestnuts like: "The schematic textual hierarchy signified by the author-as-observed is artifactually reductive," and many more!

Order #33-90455 $8.95

Life's Little Indestructible Book: In the old West, cowboys relied on their breast-pocket bibles to stop speeding bullets. Today, you need even greater protection. This book of daily affirmations, made of thousands of layers of micro-bonded Mylar sheeting, is full of good advice for living and tough enough to deflect a .45 caliber bullet at point blank range.

Order #38-01424 $650.00

Life's Microscopic Instruction Book: The world's smallest self-help book, this marvel of modern technology offers 220 pages of inspirational quotations, exhortations, and meditations in a volume so small you could fit the entire first print run on the head of a pin! Comes complete with DNA-strand bookmark and The Itty Bitty Teeny Weeny Book Light.

Order # 44-30321 $89.95

ten stupid things women do to mess up their hair

Dr. Laura Schippenger

Author of
YOU JUST DON'T UNDERSTAND: Women and Hairdressers in Conversation

Home Perm

Twisted Sister

Wormy Bangs

Post Break-Up Chop

Dr. Laura Schippenger, world renowned psychobeautician, is here to help us break through our denial and take responsibility for our own bad hair days. *Ten Stupid Things Women Do To Mess Up Their Hair* takes an in-depth look at case studies culled from her two decades of diagnosing, counseling, cutting, and styling. As Dr. Schippenger strips away the harsh chemicals and emotional armor, we gain insight into the attitudes that helped shape these hairtrocities, and the doctor's shrewd advice shows us how we can avoid making the same dreadful mistakes.

Mall Hair

Rod Stewart

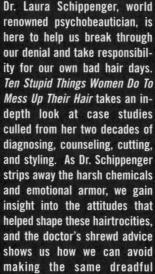

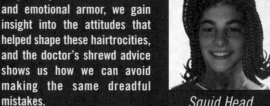

Squid Head

Cousin It

Tortuga Flats

Curly Fries

The
BEARDED
LADIES'

COMMON-SENSE
INVESTMENT
GUIDE

"Would these Street-smart sweeties steer you wrong?
Not by the hair on their chinny-chin-chin!"
– DAVE CAMINEAR, MANAGER,
RINGLING BROS. AND BARNUM & BAILEY GROWTH FUND

LOOKING for the greatest investment minds of the century? You won't find them in New York or Tokyo. But you might run into them in Gramble, Missouri. Or Sweetwater, Texas. Or Percival, Wyoming, depending on the time of year. All of these stops are on the route of the V.G. Kareken Traveling Sideshow, where, for the past 5 years, the Bearded Ladies' Investment Club has outperformed so-called market gurus by a whopping 3-to-1 margin.

These hirsute high-rollers aren't privy to any special inside information or fancy computer projections. In fact, they are on the road so much, they barely get to read the trades. But they're not too busy to keep their eyes and ears open for potential market indicators. When they noticed the Albino Family stocking up on Coppertone, they invested. When Fred and Ted, the world's fattest twins, switched from Burger King to McDonald's, they followed suit. And when the knife thrower's assistant decided upon Aetna Life Insurance, you can bet they went along for the ride.

You needn't run off and join the circus to emulate these shaggy shareholders. *The Bearded Ladies' Common Sense Investment Guide* will show you how to use your own observational skills to outsmart the market and beat the Wall Street bigwigs every time. The ladies guarantee it. In fact, if you follow their advice and don't achieve similar results, they'll not only refund your money, they'll shave!

"My portfolio is up 27% in just four months!"
– OTIS THE FROG BOY

102977 6 36 253

MEN WHO HATE WOMEN...
& WITH GOOD REASON!

THE DIVORCÉ'S GUIDE TO BITTER LIVING

DR. AUGUSTUS STRINDBERG

LIVE WITHOUT 'EM!

If you've recently suffered a painful divorce, you know how hard it can be to pick up the pieces and move on. Well, who says you have to? *Men Who Hate Women...And With Good Reason!* is the breakthrough non-recovery program that shows you how to keep the heartbreak and humiliation fresh by embracing bitterness as a lifestyle choice. The author and his panel of twelve angry men will show you how to stop blaming yourself for things that happened in the past – and start blaming her. You'll learn how to carry your spitefulness over into your relations with other women, nurturing a smoldering resentment that's the next best thing to actually feeling good!

TOPICS COVERED:

What Women Really Want: *Who Cares?*

Communication Skills: *What's the Point?*

Your Hidden Anger: *Let Her Rip!*

Building Mutual Trust: *A Likely Story.*

Get What You Want In Bed: *As If.*

Letting Down Your Guard: *A Very Bad Idea.*

About the Author: Dr. Augustus Strindberg is a thrice-divorced psychotherapist and the author of three previous relationship books: *Love Forever, Love the Second Time Around*, and *Third Time's A Charm*. He lives in Portland, Maine, with his Chihuahua, Small Consolation.

"Five years into my marriage, everything was going great. Then I read your book, and decided to chuck the whole damn thing. Thanks!"
– Orville Nugent, U.S.M.C.

$11.95

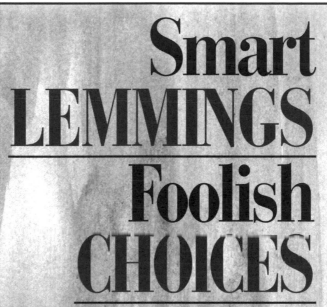

Smart
LEMMINGS
Foolish
CHOICES

THE SAVVY LEMMING'S GUIDE
TO SELF-PRESERVATION

Peggy Lemming

THIS BOOK CAN BE USED AS A FLOTATION DEVICE

BEAT THE URGE TO SUBMERGE

"Sure, I had heard the stories – but there was always a sense of, 'It can't happen to me.' Well, I found out the hard way: It can happen to any lemming, any time." – The Author

Peggy Lemming was one of the lucky ones. Washed back onto shore by a fortuitous wave, she survived that fateful day when hundreds of thousands of her friends and relatives plunged to their deaths in the icy Arctic waters. In the chilling introductory chapter, she recounts the horror of returning to the beach the following morning to find it carpeted with the water-logged carcasses of her doomed den-mates – an image that haunts her to this day.

While she still has no explanation for her behavior that horrific night, Peggy has devoted her life to informing other lemmings of the peril, in the hopes that they might be spared her terrifying experience. Sadly, many lemmings continue to ignore the reality of Sodden Lemming Death Syndrome (SLDS) despite compelling evidence, such as the absence of any senior citizens in their communities. As a result, Ms. Lemming's book has never been more valuable – or more necessary.

"A book for the masses!" – Vladimir Ilich Lemming

900 877 458456

THE DHARMA

OF THE GIFTED

CHILD

Further Teachings of the World's
Youngest Buddhist Master

by Billy Sweeny
Author of the National Scholastic Bestsellers:
Zen and the Art of Tricycle Maintenance and *The Seven Spiritual Laws of Recess*

Since becoming – at age nine – the youngest person ever to achieve the status of Buddhist Master, Billy Sweeny of Santa Clara, CA, has won international acclaim for his pioneering work in Pediatric Enlightenment. His snacktime lecture series, *Tales of a Fourth-Grader on Nothing*, has introduced millions of elementary school students to the basic tenets of Buddhism. Now, in *Dharma of the Gifted Child*, Master Sweeny provides a collection of stories, poems, and koans (spiritual riddles) designed to awaken young minds to the illusory nature of dialectical existence. Here are some examples:

Miss Lucy had a steamboat
The steamboat had a bell
The bell sounded the clear note
Of Buddha Consciousness

Banku: "Guess what?"
Disciple: "What?"
Banku: "That's what."

Solitary disciple
Sitting beneath a tree
M-E-D-I-T-A-T-I-N-G
First comes samatha [calm abiding]
Then comes vipasyana [mystical insight]
Then comes dwelling in the Sublime
  Jewel-House of the Buddha Mind

$13.50

1209 38 7711

SPANK

AND GROW

RICH

Pursuing a Career in Domination

"*A whacking good read!*"
— Lord Cuthburt Pembroke,
The London Daily Cudgel

**Sidney Biddle
Bottoms**

Leather Bound Edition

PUT YOURSELF IN A WORLD OF HURT!

Considering a career change? If you're a motivated self-starter and enjoy working with your hands, you may have what it takes to succeed in the exciting and lucrative field of professional erotic dominance. In *Spank and Grow Rich*, you'll find complete instructions on how to successfully finance, market, manage, promote, and franchise your own house of pain.

▲ NAMING THE BUSINESS: An agency name can be a powerful marketing tool – or a major disaster. Just ask Mistress Elvira, whose pricey Park Avenue agency, Spank Barn, folded within a year.

▲ LOGISTICS: Learn from the unfortunate experience of Frau Spankenstein, who signed a five-year lease before realizing her building wasn't zoned for a coal-fired Wheel of Torture.

▲ PROMOTION: Find out why Mistress Victoria was able to boost her business by offering a fixed-price "All You Can Be Beat" special; while Mistress Justine lost money on her labor-intensive "Three Martinet Lunch."

▲ NICHE MARKETING: After floundering in the mainstream market, Mistress Gertrude was able to attract a devoted client base by putting on a baker's hat, rolling her clients in flour, and doling out thirteen whacks for the price of twelve.

▲ INDEMNITY: Mistress Infinity let her medical coverage lapse, then paid the price when a client's re-enactment of *The 400 Blows* ended in a call to 911.

About the Author: *For almost two decades, Sydney Biddle Bottoms, a Mayflower descendant and Harvard MBA, has dominated the domination industry with her unique brand of stiff-handed administration. Her agency, Au Bon Pain, has grown into a multimillion dollar business with over 200 franchises in 20 countries, and is represented on major erotic stock indexes including the S&M 500 and the Ow Jones.*

"I wanted to be a stockbroker, but options for women were limited. So I figured, 'If you can't join them, beat them!'"

– MISTRESS GWEN GOLDMAN,
OWNER OF WALL STREET'S HOTTEST DUNGEON,
GOLDMAN SMACKS

697 04965 58

$15.99

$14,000 things to be happy about

THE GREEDY BOOK BY BARBARA ANN KIBITZER

$ A Rolex $

$ A bathtub full of Dom Perignon '71 $

$ Jackie O's eyebrow pencil $

$ A congressman's integrity $

$ A Tiffany diamond nose stud $

$ A week in bed with a high-class call girl $

$ 14,000 gift certificates to
Everything For A Dollar $

$ A home sensory deprivation tank $

$ Your new face $

They say money can't buy happiness, but fourteen thousand bucks sure makes a nice downpayment. Whether your riches are real or imagined, nouveau or ancestral, hard-earned or ill-gotten, you'll love the sometimes practical, often extravagant suggestions from world-renowned personal shopper Barbara Ann Kibitzer in this epic paean to unabashed consumerism.

$14.00

912 485 75756

MAKE THE CONFECTION

PLANNING THE PERFECT CONSOLATION BINGE

An Oprah's Book Club Selection!

OPRAH WINFREY

with her personal pastry chef

BART TATIN

Oprah Winfrey is back
– and she's bigger than ever!

Two years into her life-transforming collaboration with fitness guru Bob Greene, the TV mega-star and notorious yo-yo dieter seemed to have her weight problem beaten once and for all. She even teamed up with Greene to write a book, *Make The Connection*, documenting her success. But after an argument over serving sizes turned hostile, Greene unceremoniously dumped her for Sally Jesse Raphael, and a heartbroken Oprah made the connection – with a cheesecake the size of a Buick.

Now, you can treat yourself to the same decadent diet that has helped Oprah and millions of others to successfully scarf their way through the pain of a major disappointment. Co-written with her friend and pastry chef Bart Tatin, *Make the Confection* is the definitive guide to the post-rejection pork-out, filled with recipes, meal suggestions, and stories of Oprah's own difficult recovery – such as the time she stapled CBS programming executive Alan Zwellig's hand to her desk after he made an ill-advised grab for her bowl of Jordan almonds. Whether you're bouncing back from a pink slip, a breakup, or a personal humiliation, it's the simple, scrumptious way to fill that emptiness inside!

"It's not about stuffing your face –
it's about changing your life!"
— NAWANDA BANKS,
THE NAWANDA BANKS SHOW

109 98 76 772

How to Win Followers & Indoctrinate People

FOUNDING AND OPERATING YOUR OWN RELIGIOUS CULT

THE REVEREND CLEMENT SMOLTZ

If you've ever dreamed of starting your own religious mind-control movement, there's never been a better time than now, and there's never been a better book than *How To Win Followers And Indoctrinate People*. The Reverend Clement Smoltz, founder of the *Temple Of The Lord's Shoulders* in Waukegan, Illinois, provides you with all the information you'll need to ensnare, brainwash, and reprogram your loyal following.

Reverend Clem started *The Lord's Shoulders* in his mother's basement with only two followers: the family housekeeper and a German exchange student. Ten years later he has 300 followers, a cattle ranch, and a successful Web page design business, staffed completely with members of his flock. If he can do it, so can you!

In *How To Win Followers,* the good Reverend provides you with the tools for building a successful cult, and addresses the 50 most-heard complaints of new leaders, including:

- **My members keep getting abducted back by their families!**
- **I'm having trouble defining my character: Am I God, the son of God, or do I just talk to God?**
- **My airport flower business isn't pulling in what I had hoped.**
- **I've got a Doomsday cult and my followers seem anxious to "ascend." Do I have to go with them?**
- **If I adapt the "Hare Krishna" song, can I be sued?**
- **My stockpile of weapons needs beefing up.**
- **I started a Jews for Jesus group, and I have no idea what I'm talking about.**
- **Our team is the laughingstock of the Inter-Cult Softball League.**

NO MORE EXCUSES! Right now, in some small church basement, the next David Koresh is stockpiling his first AK-47, the next Jim Jones is whipping up his first batch of kool-aid, and the next Marshall Applewhite is deciding whether to use the word "castration" in his mission statement. What are YOU waiting for – the end of the world!?!

$14.99

456 823 978

GERMS DO IT. PROTOZOA DO IT. NOW YOU CAN, TOO!

My
MOTHER
MYSELF

A Guide to Asexual Reproduction

NANCY "TWOFER" TUESDAY
author of *The Joy of Asex*

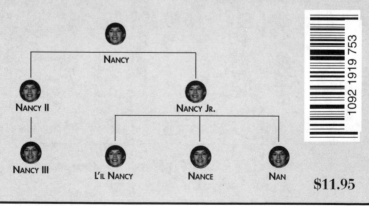

SIX WEEKS TO WORDS OF POWER LIFTERS

Communicate With The Massive

By Famed Sports Linguist
LARS HEINRICH

"RRRRAAAARRRRRGGGGGHHHHH!"
— PETE CORRALIS, U.S. BENCH PRESS CHAMPION

YOU SEE THEM IN THE FREEWEIGHTS SECTION OF THE GYM, sweating and grunting and bashing their chests together. Everything about them is exotic, from their language to their clothing to their Herculean displays of strength. You want to talk to them, but you're afraid that they will misunderstand you and crush your skull like a lima bean.

Fear no more! Famed sports linguist Lars Heinrich has blasted through the communication barrier with the first ever English-to-Powerlifter phrasebook and vocabulary builder. Organized to make learning as easy as a 10-pound dumbbell squat, the book provides dozens of games and exercises focusing on the key words, phrases and idioms you'll need when travelling through downtown Barbaria. If you stick with the program and do your reps, you'll have a vocab of steel in just 6 weeks!

GENERAL WEIGHTROOM CONVERSATION:
How would you reply when one of your huge friends asks "GRELCH!?!" (Are you using that bench?) And what happens if they intone "FLLAAR-RGH!!" (Hand me the chalk.) And if they really take a liking to you, they may enlist you to "FRRAACCKK!!" (Help me find a vein.)

EATS AND DRINKS:
Create A Popular Powerlifter Beverage Using Any Three
Of These Words (Hint: There are no wrong answers.)

Turbo	Carbo	Mega	Super
Power	Amino	Boost	Bulk
Juice	Mass	Fuel	2000

SPOTTERSPEAK:
Practice enunciating these phrases as fast
and as loud as you can.
"You got it! You got it! You got it! You got it!"
"All you!!! All you!!! All you!!! All you!!! All you!!!"

KEVIN TRUDEAU'S
MEGA MAMMARY

From the world's foremost authority on
psychodynamic mammary enhancement

Let the Power of Inflational Thinking Give You the Devastating Decolletage of Your Dreams!

"Your bust will boom!" - REDBOOB

Make Mountains out of Molehills...
Or Your Money Back!

Ladies! Are you short a few pence in the pectoral piggy banks? Singing a bit flat at the Casaba Cabaret? Running your bazoom box on AAA batteries? Let's face it: When it comes to attracting a mate, small-chested women know all too well that the deck is stacked against them – and in favor of the stacked!

But now you can have the bountiful clavicular frontage you've always dreamed about – without invasive surgery, costly drugs, or unsightly cup-stuffing. In *Mega Mammary*, Kevin Trudeau, President of the American Mammary Institute at Bazonga University, shows you how to unlock your breasts' hidden potential through a process of directed visualization, meditation, and simple exercises you can do in the privacy of your own home. You'll notice results after just a few weeks of practice; and in three months, you'll be reaping a hefty harvest of multiplied mammiferous mass! Why not start building your future today?

"Pack your things, girls – Mega Mammary is your one-way ticket from Flatbush to Cleaveland!"

– NAWANDA BANKS,
  THE NAWANDA BANKS SHOW

Give us
a week –
We'll put on
the tits!

This book was funded in part by a grant from the Melon Foundation

THIN THIGHS FOR 30 BUCKS

by Marty Millner

Save big with do-it-yourself home plastic surgery!

From the Time/Life Home
Self-Improvement Series

Considering cosmetic surgery, but can't justify the high cost? Now you can have the look you want for far less than you'd pay at one of those expensive "professional" clinics. Let Marty Millner, host of the hit PBS show *This Old Face*, guide you step-by-step through 50 exciting and inexpensive home self-improvement projects that will leave you and your whole family looking terrific!

Procedure:	What You'll Need:	Time To Complete:	Your Cost:
Liposuction	Dust Buster, 3 plastic flexi-straws, pen light, hole punch	20 minutes per pound of fat	$35.25
Breast Augmentation	2 Ziploc Bags, 1 box instant pudding mix, box cutter, shoehorn, duct tape	15 minutes per breast plus 1 hour for pudding.	$22.75
Face Lift	8 safety pins, 1 tube super glue, marking pencil, pinking shears	45 minutes	$18.75
Nose Job	Mallet, vegetable peeler, carpenter's putty, Q-Tips	30 minutes plus 2 hours for putty to dry	$27.95
Hair Replacement	Toupee, staple gun	2 minutes	$35.20

 "After twenty years of neglect, my wife and I were looking pretty rundown and shabby. We called in a private contractor, but the estimate came to over $11,000. So I got Marty's book, and did all the renovations myself for just $211.28. The wife's looking great, I'm looking great, and people have really noticed the difference! Tomorrow we start on the kids!"
— GEORGE HAYDEN, MIDFIELD CT

$13.50

9685 4857

ABSOLUTE POWER

Anthony Robbins

For almost two decades, Anthony Robbins, the world's most successful motivational speaker and creator of the 25-million copy best-selling audiocassette series Personal Power, *has encouraged people to lead extraordinary lives. Now he's insisting.*

RESISTANCE IS FUTILE

On January 1, 2000, responding to a subliminal message inserted into Tony's *Personal Power* tapes, tens of millions of people will suddenly leave their homes and offices and rise up in a single unified force and take over the world. Once Earth has been conquered, Tony will appear in a special TV infomercial during which he will announce the dissolution of all existing governments and their replacement with his United Republic of Peak Performance (URPP).

As Benevolent Overlord For Life of URPP, Tony will insist that his citizens constantly work to actualize their full human potential and live life to the fullest, or face incarceration in one of Tony's maximum security Gulags of Personal Empowerment. An elaborate network of surveillance equipment, informants, and undercover security operatives will monitor Tony's populace twenty-four hours a day to ensure that they remain confident and free of self-defeating behavior patterns.

There is no stopping Tony and his followers; they are far too motivated, energized, and goal-oriented to be denied. *Absolute Power* tells you what you need to know to survive and thrive in the glorious Personal Power Paradise of the 21st Century.

$15.98

"She makes shoplifting uplifting!"
– HOT COUTURE

HOW TO LOOK LIKE A MILLION

Without Spending A Dime

HILLARY SIMON
Author of EUROPE ON NO DOLLARS A DAY

Make No Payments - Ever!

> **"Buy a woman a blouse, you clothe her for a day; teach her how to steal a blouse, you clothe her for a lifetime."**

If you're ready to say goodbye to the dehumanizing tasks of coupon-clipping, comparison shopping, and waiting in long check-out lines, *How To Look Like A Million Without Spending A Dime* can help you look and feel great without maxing out your credit cards in the process. This theft-provoking book has already motivated thousands of women to make the switch from fashion victim to fashionable felon, showing them the true meaning of the saying, "The Lord helps those who help themselves."

After reviewing basic shoplifting technique, Simon will take you on a "field trip" where you'll have to negotiate a floor plan, create a diversion, give security the slip, avoid the fitting room camera, and exit cleanly through an electronic theft-deterrence system with an ermine muff stuffed down your knickers. Once you've mastered these simple moves, you're on your way to unlimited credit at the world's largest storewide clearance sale.

Tools of the Trade

Hollow beehive haircut

Rear-view glasses for security detection

Giant removable shoulder pads

Demagnetization belt buckle

Trap-door purse

"I'm preggers" inflatable stomach

Skirt with hidden loot hammock

False bottom platform shoes

$19.95

2074 586 32746

The writing was excellent – terse yet playful; economical but not at all dry. Perfect for enjoying with a frisky red such as a Chianti or a Côtes du Rhone. "

— GAEL VERDIGRIS, THE INSUFFERABLE GOURMET

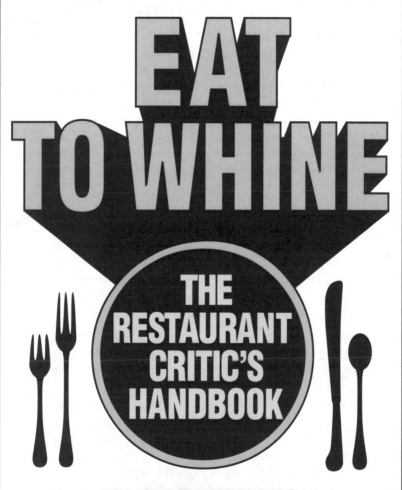

EAT TO WHINE

THE RESTAURANT CRITIC'S HANDBOOK

EDWARD MUNCH

IF YOU ENJOY

dining out and you love to complain, you already
have the basic qualifications to succeed in one of America's
cushiest fields: Professional Restaurant Criticism. No matter what your
current level of culinary expertise, *Eat to Whine* can help you develop
the skills, knowledge, and attitude you need to parlay your interests
in crapulence and nitpicking into a fruitful career on the
glutting edge of journalism.

Even if you don't know Spago from Sbarros or Paul Bocuse from
Paul Prudhomme, *Eat to Whine* can equip you with
the expertise you need to discourse passionately
and *ad nauseam* on everything from correct taramos-
alata temperature to appropriate sommelier attire to the
relative merits of the Madagascar vs. the Indonesian vanilla
bean. It won't be long before you're appointing yourself the
sole arbiter of culinary excellence, monopolizing table conversation with your tedious editorializing, and describing
yourself as "a confirmed foodie."

Competition for jobs in restaurant criticism is fierce, but new positions
are constantly opening up as existing critics drop dead from overindul-
gence. To give you the inside track on such profitable and profligate
employment, *Eat to Whine* will show you how to turn your knowledge
of culinary trivia into a gushing river of purple prose that editors of
gourmet food magazines will find irresistible. You'll also get the
invaluable *Eat to Whine Style Guide*, packed with useful
references, including 32 synonyms for "delicious,"
235 snooty wine adjectives, and a cross-indexed
Garnish Identification Chart.

ALL I KNOW I LEARNED IN KINDERGARTEN

◇

Surviving the
Effects of
a Childhood
Head Injury

◇

ROBERT FULGUMP
as told to Helmut Vögler

Dunderhead
PRESS

"*My name is Robert Fulgump. People call me Robert Fulgump.*"

Thrown from a donkey at his fifth birthday party, Robert Fulgump's neurological development was permanently halted at the kindergarten level. This book is the story of his struggles, setbacks, and ultimate success as an inspirational speaker and author, as told to his friend and personal dresser, Helmut Vögler.

"People like Mr. Fulgump should serve as alarms for the rest of us to get off our duffs and live, live, live!!!"
– Nawanda Banks,
   The Nawanda Banks Show

Also by the same author:
It Lay Down When I Set Fire To It 🍎

343 99 876 3737

$13.95

Stuff Your Face with Fat and Carbs

Gorge Yourself on Grease and Cheese

EAT THE CALZONE

A DIETARY ROAD MAP TO

✔ **BUILD A BIGGER, MORE IMPRESSIVE GUT**

✔ **ADD JIGGLE TO YOUR UPPER ARMS AND THIGHS**

✔ **EXPAND YOUR BUTTOCK VOLUME BY UP TO 300%**

✔ **INCREASE YOUR CAPACITY FOR THUNDEROUS FLATULENCE**

✔ **DEVELOP EXCITING NEW CHINS**

BY EDWARD DUPOIS

Put the Power of The CalZone to Work For You!

Whether you're professionally portly or just recreationally obese, you need to know about *The CalZone*, the amazing new diet technology that can help you put on all the weight you want – and keep it on!

Developed by researchers in applied calzonics at Vito's Pizzeria and Institute of Technology, The CalZone Diet involves carefully targeted manipulation of your body's hormones to promote maximum fat retention; yet the regimen is remarkably simple to follow. A calzone for breakfast, another for mid-morning snack, another for elevenses, another for lunch, another for early-afternoon snack, another for high tea, another for happy hour, and a sensible dinner are all you need to start living large and feeling great big!

Who Can Benefit from Eating The CalZone?

✔ **DEPARTMENT STORE SANTAS:**
"I was a 97-pound weakling, and it made me a laughingstock. Kids used to fall off my lap; the other Santas called me 'Old Saint Stick.' One day, a burly elf walked up and flicked fake snow in my face, and I decided I'd had enough. I put myself on the CalZone Diet and by the following Christmas, I'd gained 250 pounds of pure, rippling fat. It really works!"

– S.N., Marietta, GA

✔ **OPERA SINGERS:**
"My voice coach told me I needed to gain 150 pounds to be able to belt out those big, buttery cadenzas like a pro. Try as I might, though, I just couldn't put on the weight. Finally, a friend of mine who is a plus-sized model introduced me to *The CalZone*. I gained 182 pounds in three months, and next July this fat lady sings at the Met!"

– J.M.B., Lexington, MA

✔ **ELVIS IMPERSONATORS:**
"When I got hired by Caesar's to play the 1970's Elvis in their floor show, I had no idea how kingsize the King had become. *The Calzone* made me man enough to fill out His Majesty's XXX-Large rhinestone-studded spandex bodysuit."

– T.P., Las Vegas, NV

298765 20986

$11.95

More Than 16,000,000 Souls Sold
HAVE THE ACTING CAREER
DAMIENETICS
YOU'VE ALWAYS DREAMED OF
"Signing with one bad man got me A Few Good Men."
–Tom Cruise
PUBLISHED BY
The Church of Satanology

GET ON BOARD WITH THE UNDERLORD!

Why don't agents return my calls?
READ THE BOOK
Why are mediocre actors getting all the work?
READ THE BOOK
Why am I still slinging hash at the local IHOP?
READ THE BOOK

If you're a performer and you find yourself asking any of these questions, you need to find out about the most powerful force in Hollywood today. His company, **ICM (International Chthonic Management)**, has struck more blockbuster deals than **CAA** and William Morris combined. He is so potent, so savvy, so well-connected, He makes talent and training virtually obsolete. And if He's not working for you, He's most definitely working against you. Isn't it about time you joined His team?

Damienetics, published by the Church of Satanology (West), contains all the materials you'll need to jumpstart your stalled acting career, including contracts, projected time lines and the **ICM** comprehensive benefits package. Peruse the information at your leisure. Make sure you understand all the fine points of the agreement. Once executed, it is binding in perpetuity.

Once you've signed the contracts and recited the secret incantation, Lucifer will reveal himself to you in the form of a superagent, holding a gram of coke and a three-picture deal. Congratulations are in order. You're on your way to the career of your dreams.

"After Urban Cowboy, *my career pretty much sputtered. Then a friend gave me Damienetics. I read it, recited my incantation, and lo! An agent appeared unto me. A week later I was cast in* Pulp Fiction, *and the rest has been gravy."*
— John Travolta

666

The COMPLETE and UTTER
IDIOT'S
Guide to
Life
John Simpleton
Duh-HUH!
Quick and easy ways to reduce your "ignorance quotient"
Idiot-proof steps for making the most of your crouton-sized brain
Valuable tips for getting by when you're as stupid as the day is long
HENRY DOLT PUBLISHING

Hey, Idiot!

Yes, we're talking to you, chucklehead. Listen. You didn't ask to be born an idiot. And just because you happen to have the mental acuity of a lichen and an IQ measured in points above prime, that's no reason why you shouldn't be able to live a happy and fulfilling life. Unfortunately, you're so monumentally dense, you probably don't have any idea how to go about it.

Take heart, cretin! *The Complete And Utter Idiot's Guide To Life* is jam-packed with useful advice for mental defectives just like yourself, written in easy-to-understand sentences and printed in large type on specially-coated drool-proof paper. Inside, we'll provide detailed instructions telling you how to do even the simplest things, including:

- Walk and Chew Gum at the Same Time
- Tell Your Ass From a Hole in the Ground
- Count to Twenty Without Removing Your Shoes
- Think Your Way Out of a Paper Bag

The Complete And Utter Idiot's Guide To Life is truly a book any idiot could benefit from. Indeed, the book is so useful, you'd be an idiot *not* to buy it... but don't let that stop you.

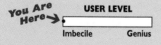

You Are Here →

USER LEVEL

Imbecile   Genius

Stupid People Read Idiot's Guides:

"The information is presented in a very simple and straightforward style. I had no trouble getting it through my thick skull." — Annie Dullard, author of *Pinhead At Tinker Creek*

"I'm telling all my idiot friends!" — Ignoramos Oz, author of *Stupid Is As Stupid Does: A Memoir*

About the Author: *John Simpleton is the Alfred North Wafflehead Professor of Idiotics at Carbozo University, and author of best-selling idiot self-help books, including:* You Mean I'm Not Lazy Or Crazy — Just Stupid? *and* Drawing On The Only Side Of The Brain

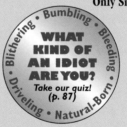

Blithering • Bumbling • Bleeding • Natural-Born • Driveling

WHAT KIND OF AN IDIOT ARE YOU?
Take our quiz!
(p. 87)

EASY-TO-USE-ICONS

⊂ Read it again, idiot!

(!) Bonehead alert!

2356 567 121

$16.95

Cats Are from Saturn

DOGS ARE FROM PLUTO

A Practical Guide for Improving
Communication With the Opposite Pet

JOHN GRAY, Ph.D.

Cats Are from Saturn

Dogs hate cats. Cats hate dogs. That's just the way it is, and it will never change...Or could it?

In this provocative sequel to his best-selling relationship book, *Men are from Mars, Women are from Venus*, Dr. John Gray explores the deep-seated fears, instinctual suspicions, and inter-species misunderstandings that exist between dogs and cats, and the way in which they interfere with the development of mutually fulfilling inter-pet relationships.

TOPICS ILLUMINATED

Whose Ball Is It Anyway?
OWNERSHIP IN A COMMUNITY ENVIRONMENT

I'm Neutered, You're Not
DEALING WITH ISSUES OF LOVE AND LOSS

Don't Pee on My Scratching Post
SETTING AND RESPECTING BOUNDARIES

We Can BOTH Wreck the X-Mas Tree
COOPERATION VS. INDIVIDUAL INITIATIVE

Our Common Enemy – The Vacuum Cleaner
MOVING BEYOND "FIGHT OR FLIGHT"

The Master's Lap
OVERCOMING DEPENDENCY ON THE "SIGNIFICANT OWNER"

Baby Makes Three
CURBING THE "MAUL" INSTINCT

DOGS ARE FROM PLUTO

$11.95

PORKERS OF THE WORLD – UNITE!

CHAIRMAN ATKINS' GLORIOUS DIET REVOLUTION

THE BREAKTHROUGH DIET REGIME THAT HAS FREED MILLIONS FROM THE YOKE OF IMPERIALIST GLUTTONY

THE DIET REVOLUTION WILL NOT BE TELEVISED

COMRADES! The time has come to throw off
the shackles of the bourgeois diet ideology and forge a bold
new weight-loss plan for the modern proletariat, free from the
excesses of corpulent capitalism and mass consumption.
Through strict adherence to Chairman Atkins' dietary dogma
combined with periodic purging, you'll rise up and overthrow
the rich foods, depose the oppressor fat cells, and jettison the
satellite states of cellulite and cholesterol.

Under the lean, muscular arm of the diet revolution, you
will gain membership to the People's Health and Fitness
Cooperative, where you will participate in Collectivized
Firming on the Trot-Ski machines and work out to the "Iron
Curtain Abs" video. You will also receive a copy of *The Little
Red Cookbook*, which includes such revolutionary recipes as
Imperialist Swine, Bass Kapital, K. G. Beef, and Pol Pot Pie.

ATKINS' MAXIMS

| To each according to his metabolism | Carbohydrates are the opiates of the massive |

"LONG LIVE THE GLORIOUS DIET REVOLUTION
AND OUR BELOVED LEADER, CHAIRMAN ATKINS!"
— Terrence Malshevick, director,
The Thin Red Waistline

WHEN BAD THINGS HAPPEN TO GOOD HUMOR PEOPLE

"I SCREAM, YOU SCREAM, WE ALL SCREAM AT THE INJUSTICES OF LIFE, BUT THESE BRAVE VENDORS FACE ADVERSITY WITH REMARKABLE FORTITUDE."

-- Edmund Claire, host of
A Dairy Home Companion

ROBIN BASKINS, Ph.D.

Inspirational Firsthand Accounts

They ply their trade on the sidestreets and thoroughfares of America, armed only with a strong sense of spirituality and a scoop. They are Good Humor people, and here they talk candidly about their darkest moments and deepest fears on the front lines of their ice cream routes.

"A bunch of hooligans locked me in my own freezer. It was only for a couple of minutes, but at the time I thought, 'This could be it.' I made a cross out of popsicle sticks and prayed."
— JEFFREY BENOIT, FAYERVILLE, IN

"There I was, with a line of 13 kids waiting there at the beach, and my change belt jams up. I couldn't get anything — quarters, dimes or nickels. I had to act quickly. I unloaded all the change into my pockets and counted it out by hand. Luckily, I had been trained both ways."
— MARY WHITE, MIAMI, FL

"Sometimes the music drives me crazy. That 'Pop Goes The Weasel' over and over and over. It can make you mental, that 'Pop Goes The Weasel.' You get destructive thoughts."
— STEVE GIBBS, QUEENS, NY

"It was barely noon, and I had run out of Fudgicles, Creamsicles, and Toasted Almonds. The children were angry. I thought, 'In this situation, what would Mohammed do?' Then I saw the Peace Pops."
— ALI MAMOUN-DIDI, WORCESTER, MA

"I drive the third shift. It gets pretty lonely, especially during winter. There are no kids around. Most of my clients are hookers on break and junkies trying to get a Fudgicle fix. One night this drug dealer comes by, all beat up. Somebody had jumped him. I gave him an Italian Ice to put over his eye."
— CHRIS MAZZILLI, WASHINGTON, D.C.

445 99 801187

$9.95

By Mary McFurgle,
Director of Women's Studies, Texas A&M

WOMEN WHO LOVE TO MULCH

"McFurgle despises the patriarchy, and she knows how deep to plant a bean!"
– Equal Rights and Gardens

The Feminist Gardening Guide

♀ ✿ ♀ ✿ ♀ ✿ ♀ ✿ ♀ ✿ ♀ ✿ ♀ ✿ ♀ ✿ ♀ ✿ ♀

Do you rail against the marginalization of women perpetuated by the patriarchal belief system of the male power structure? Do you dream of a society in which a woman's sexual identity is not held hostage to the externally-imposed imagery of heterosexist mass culture? Do your crocuses come up crooked? Then this is the book for you.

Women Who Love to Mulch is the first gardening book written exclusively for the woman with a raised fist and a green thumb. Whether you're trimming hedges or battling male hegemony, you'll love the useful tips, upbeat quips, and angry poetry in this dispatch from the front lines of the horticulture wars.

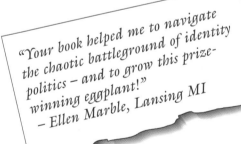

"Your book helped me to navigate the chaotic battleground of identity politics – and to grow this prize-winning eggplant!"
– Ellen Marble, Lansing MI

$10.95

101977 61 16622

LET'S GO

THE BUDGET TRAVELER'S GUIDE

HELL

INCLUDING PURGATORY & LIMBO

"The best guide to Hell since Dante's Inferno!"
– *BELOW!* MAGAZINE

HELL, YES!

Mythical kingdom of Hades and Persephone; sulfurous abode of the eternally damned; inspiration for artists from Goethe to Sartre – Hell is a place of myriad fascinations for the budget-minded tourist. *Let's Go: Hell* tells you everything you need to plan and enjoy an exciting vacation to tarnation – without having to sell your soul to pay for it.

- **Preparation:** There's rarely a cold day in Hell, so pack light (and flame-retardant) – we'll tell you how.
- **Accommodations:** Take your pick from our list of budget-oriented Hell holes.
- **Local Entertainment:** We list hundreds of fun-filled activities, from junior prom re-enactments to dueling Nirvana tribute bands to improvisational epileptic synchronized swimming, and more!
- **Festivals:** Catch all seven days of hazing during Hell Week.
- **Tourist Attractions:** Spend the day at DMV World, visit the Hitler exhibit at the Hell Hall of Fame, or hear Hell's Bells ringing in the Black Mass at the Cathedrale de Notre Damn.

★★★
Traveler's Tip:
Don't pay the
ferry man until
he gets you to
the other side!

- **The Arts:** From Hell's number-one sitcom, *I Love Lucifer*, to big-budget musicals (*Damned Yankees; Hell, Dolly!*), to current cinema (*Desperately Seeking Satan*), we'll tell you what's hot.
- **Gyms:** Check out the Endless StairMaster and all the other equipment down at Sissyphus Health and Fitness!
- **Restaurants:** Stop in at any of the fine eateries in Hell's Kitchen for top-notch devil dogs, deviled eggs, devil's food cake, and all-you-can-eat microwave haggis.
- **Shopping:** Find bargains on souvenir pitchforks, never-fail lighters, hair shirts, and more!

"When clients demand a first-class vacation at rock-bottom prices, I tell them: 'Go to Hell!'"
— ART MUSHNER, MUSHNER TRAVEL

NOTE: Due to circumstances beyond our control, all listings in Let's Go: Hell become out-of-date the second they are published. We regret any inconvenience.

109 9393 87

$9.99

★ Angry? Get in line! ★

For centuries, people have been using dance as a way to work out their anger and hostility. Unfortunately, the therapeutic effects of dance have proven elusive to the millions of white folks who couldn't hoof their way out of a burlap sack. Now there's a solution! Line dancing requires no coordination or rhythm whatsoever. You only need to move one body part at a time, and if you get lost, just copy the person next to you. It couldn't get any easier!

In <u>The Line Dance of Anger</u>, Charlene Bangle presents special customized versions of popular line dances, clinically proven to cool your jets and lower your blood pressure. So next time you're angry, don't pick a fight ... pick a dance, from one of these all-time favorites:

Achy Breaky of Annoyance
Macarena of Malice
Electric Slide of Irritation
Hokey-Pokey of Hostility
Tush Push of Ill Will
Boot Scootin' Boogie of Rage
Hora of Tsuris
Chicken Dance of Angst
Texas Two-Step of Disgust
Bunnyhop of Bile
Cotton-Eyed Joe of Passive-Aggressiveness

"Nowadays, when I feel a bout of domestic abuse comin' on, I just hightail it over to the local juke joint."

– JAD PLUMBER, MIDLAND, WY

7968 3764 276

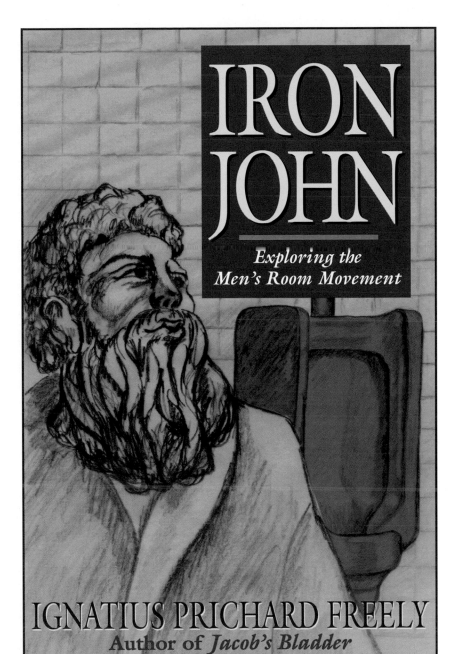

IRON JOHN

Exploring the Men's Room Movement

IGNATIUS PRICHARD FREELY

Author of *Jacob's Bladder*

Iggy Freely, Protestant minister and leader of the burgeoning Men's Room Movement, remembers the moment he discovered the link between public urination and male bonding:

I was taking a warm bath at the time. I lay there in the tub, drinking lite beer after lite beer while pondering the primal events that shape relationships among men. All at once, the insight spilled over into consciousness. I jumped up and shouted, "Urea!"

That evening, Freely composed a 20-page pamphlet, *Stand and Deliver*, outlining his key beliefs. Before long, his urinary tract began to receive exposure in the media, and the Reverend found himself in demand as a public speaker, conducting Men's Room seminars and weekend retreats at highway rest stops nationwide.

In his seminars, Freely points out that, while women understand the importance of the restroom as a social venue, men still view a trip to the toilet as a solitary pilgrimage. "Their flies may be down, but their guards remain up," he explains, "and the opportunity to achieve real intimacy is lost." In *Iron John*, he draws upon psychology, myth, and personal experience, to promote a vision of the Men's Room as a domain of male community and conviviality – a Sanctum Sanitorum in which men stand side-by-side, driven by a common need and focused on a common purpose.

Ultimately, Freely sees his mission as one of consciousness-raising, not education. He encourages men to open their minds before they open their trousers – in his memorable words, to "Tune In, Turn On, Whip Out." Only when they have reached this higher-level consciousness, he argues, will Men's Room patrons be capable of experiencing true relief.

"Freely takes aim and hits his mark! ...He releases a steady stream of insight, and squeezes every last drop from his material!"
– ROY L. SLOAN, FRATERNAL ORDER
   OF EVOLVED UROLOGISTS

$11.95

008 98 12322

THE RULER

4 5 6 7

21 20 19 18 17 16 15 14 13 2

Time-tested Secrets
for Predicting
Whether Mr. Right
Will Measure Up

◆ ◆ ◆

BE A RULER GIRL!

SIZE MATTERS!!

*L*et's face it, girls: Say what you want about the motion of the ocean, the best way to enjoy it is from onboard a big ship. But how do you know if that cute guy in accounting is floating a luxury liner or an inflatable dinghy? What if, underneath those sassy silk boxers, Mr. Right turns out to be Mr. Mite? Wouldn't it be great if you could know in advance whether, in the restaurant of love, he'll be serving up egg rolls or Tootsie Rolls, baguettes or bread sticks, gherkins or kosher dills?

Help has arrived! In *The Ruler*, you'll find dozens of proven yardsticks to help you know if you're dating Big Ben or Tiny Tim, Stuart Little or Peter The Great, including:

- **WRISTS, TOES, THUMBS, NOSE:** *Taking Advantage of Early Indicators*
- **ETHNICITY:** *Is It True What They Say?*
- **CAR-RELATIONS:** *The Bigger the Engine, the Smaller the Stick Shift*
- **TATTLETALE TIES:** *How's It Hanging?*
- **WORKING THE NETWORK:** *Can His Exes Be Trusted? How About His Mom?*
- **CONCEALED VIDEO:** *A Last Resort*

"The Ruler *helped me lose 4 inches... my fiancé!!*"
    –R.B. Tuscan, AR

"Pack your things, girls – The Ruler is your one-way ticket from Short Hills to Long Island."
    –Nawanda Banks,
    The Nawanda Banks Show

SPONTANEOUS HECKLING

BERATE YOUR WAY TO BETTER HEALTH

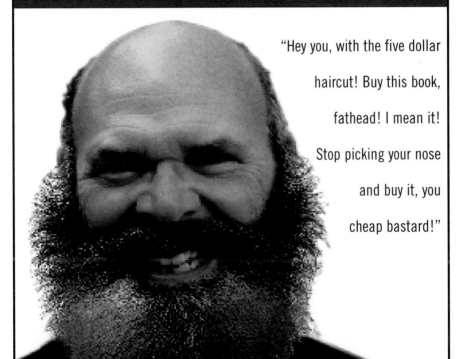

"Hey you, with the five dollar haircut! Buy this book, fathead! I mean it! Stop picking your nose and buy it, you cheap bastard!"

ANDREW VILE

"Not bad for an egg-headed, shrub-faced, buck-toothed blowhard!"
— Don Rickles, Comedian and Public Nuisance

Whether you know it or not, heckling can be

an important key to your emotional well-being. Not only does it release pent up anger and aggression, but it also triggers the flow of mood-elevating amino acids into the bloodstream. Unfortunately, most people are too timid or too civil to drop their inhibitions and let the invective fly.

If you're still squelching your exclamatory urges, radio celebrity Andrew Vile is here to help. In *Spontaneous Heckling*, Vile prescribes an eight week program consisting of open mic comedy, community theater, Mets games, and karaoke bars, designed to fill you up with so much venomous bile that the heckles will spew forth spontaneously from your very core. Once you've experienced "breakthrough," you'll feel a sense of clarity and well-being that requires only minimal weekly maintenance to sustain.

FEELING UNCREATIVE? *SPONTANEOUS HECKLING* PROVIDES YOU WITH CUSTOM-MADE BARBS FOR EVERY SITUATION:

COURT APPEARANCES: **Hang it up, gavel boy!**

AA MEETINGS: **Sit down, you lush!**

ART OPENINGS: **Who puked in the frame!**

PAPAL ADDRESSES: **Your Mother Superior!**

POETRY READINGS: **I got your Longfellow – right here!**

UNEMPLOYMENT LINES: **Don't quit your day job!**

NATIVITY PLAYS: **Where's Judas when you need him?**

MURDER MYSTERY DINNERS: **No shit, Sherlock!**

WINE TASTINGS: **Beau-jo-yo-mama!**

DOG SHOWS: **The schnauzer's got worms!**

RENAISSANCE FAIRS: **No jouster! No jouster! No jouster!**

About the Author: Andrew Vile has been thrown out of hundreds of comedy clubs, theatres and sporting events across the country. He is the host of the nationally syndicated radio talk show, "All Things Inconsiderate."

1029 8383 221187

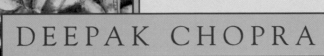

DEEPAK CHOPRA

The
SEVEN
SPIRITUAL
DWARVES
OF
SUCCESS

YOUR FAIRY TALE
GUIDE TO
FINANCIAL FREEDOM

The Dwarf of Pure Potentiality

The Dwarf of Giving

The Dwarf of Karma

The Dwarf of Least Effort

The Dwarf of Intention and Desire

The Dwarf of Detachment

Sneezy

HEIGH-HO! HEIGH-HO!

IT'S OFF TO spiritual advancement and increased income-generating potential you'll go, when you open yourself up to the wisdom of the *Seven Spiritual Dwarves of Success* who reside within us all. Let esteemed New Age success guru Deepak Chopra – author of *Bullish on Buddha* and *Dharma for Dollars* – help you translate the time-less wisdom of the classic fairy tale, *Snow White*, into quick financial gain. With Chopra as your guide, you'll learn how to sidestep the Wicked Stepmother of wrong thinking, resist the Poison Apple of ego-attachment, kiss the Handsome Prince of success conscious-ness, and live Wealthily Ever After™!

"I'd like to thank all the little people who made my success possible."
- KRIS KRINGLE, author of
SECRETS OF ELF-EMPLOYMENT

$13.95

the
CON ARTIST'S WAY

*A Swindler's
Path to
Higher Creativity*

DAN SHARP
author of
THE VEIN OF PYRITE

YOU CAN BE A PROFESSIONAL CON ARTIST IN JUST SEVEN DAYS!!!

And if you believe that, we've got an authentic, uncirculated seventeenth-century Spanish doubloon to sell you. The reality is that there are no shortcuts to gaining proficiency as a grifter – before you can give others the business, you've got to learn it yourself.

If you're serious about mastering the art of the raw deal, *The Con Artist's Way* can help. Inside, you'll find exercises and affirmations to start your deceitful juices flowing, plus plenty of practical information to get you out and chiseling as quickly as possible. Whether you're pulling a multimillion dollar bank scam or just bilking a lonely widow out of her life's savings, you'll have the skills and confidence you need to "Take 'em for all they're worth!"

Commercial Bank Loans: How to succeed in business without really owning one.

Insurance Scams: The perks and perils of leaping in front of slow-moving cars.

Brokerage Swindles: Learn the tricks of the traders. ("Don't buy, sell high.")

Televangelism: There's one born again every minute!

Pyramid Schemes: Bilk like an Egyptian.

Defective Merchandise: When life gives you lemons, sell them at a 600% markup!

About the Author: Dan Sharp, a professional con artist, author, and inspirational speaker, is the founder of the Sharp Foundation, a not-for-profit organization devoted to caring for elderly, terminally ill, homeless, orphaned children in famine regions. If you'd like to make a donation to support Dan in his tireless crusade, simply fill out the credit card information on the enclosed tear-out form and drop it in the mail. (Don't forget to sign!)

298765 20986

~~$79.99~~

$19.95!

Limbering to Prozac

The Feel-Good Workout!

"After twelve weeks of Limbering to Prozac, *I haven't lost a single pound – and I feel fantastic!"*

— MONICA BOWELS,
SIOUX CITY, IOWA

Peter D. Pressman

No Pain, No Gain – No Problem!

Tired of overhyped diet-and-exercise fads that promise amazing results but deliver only frustration and disappointment? Sick of spending long, grueling hours in the gym in a futile quest to achieve some unrealistic, media-generated ideal of physical perfection? Let pharmacist-turned-fitness-guru Peter Pressman show you how to medicate your way to a healthier, more balanced lifestyle – one dose at a time! All you need to get started is an open mind and a physician with a liberal prescription policy.

You'll notice results within a couple of weeks as the powerful seratonin reuptake inhibitors go to work, washing away feelings of insecurity, inadequacy, and discouragement, and replacing them with a diffuse yet palpable sense of well-being that lasts and lasts. Your workouts will seem easier, because they'll *be* easier – a whopping 50% easier, on average! You'll be amazed at how much of your regular routine will seem superfluous once you no longer really give a damn what you look like. So grab a copy of *Limbering to Prozac* today – satisfaction is guaranteed.*

"At first, I wasn't sure that Limbering to Prozac *was right for me, but now I'm hooked!"*

– Jim Watts, Bethesda, MD

"Your program got me off the bicycle and onto the tricyclics – and all I can say is, 'Thanks!'"

– Estelle Darnell, Santa Barbara, CA

*If, after one month on *Limbering to Prozac*, you do not feel completely satisfied, return the book with the original store receipt and we will replace it with our alternative fitness guide, *Aerobicizing to Crack*.

U.S. $11.95
Can $14.95

09856 3784744

DON'T SWEAT
THE SMALL STUFF...
and It's All Small Stuff!

Simple Ways
to Keep the Little Things
in Life from
Undermining Your Dictatorship

SADDAM HUSSEIN

The Mother Of All Self-Help Books

It's no official state secret that running a brutal, repressive dictatorship can be stressful! The daily routine of shuttling between bunkers and safe houses, organizing "spontaneous" demonstrations against American imperialism, plotting to build weapons of mass destruction, and ordering the torture and execution of dissidents is enough to make even the most cold-blooded and methodical of tyrants go a little "bonkers!" In *Don't Sweat The Small Stuff*, Saddam Hussein shares 100 simple meditations that will help you to keep an iron grip on your desperate, terrorized population — and on your own sanity!

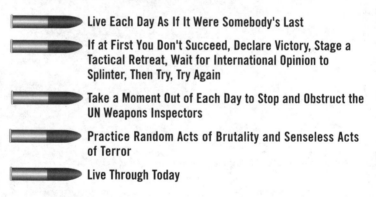

Live Each Day As If It Were Somebody's Last

If at First You Don't Succeed, Declare Victory, Stage a Tactical Retreat, Wait for International Opinion to Splinter, Then Try, Try Again

Take a Moment Out of Each Day to Stop and Obstruct the UN Weapons Inspectors

Practice Random Acts of Brutality and Senseless Acts of Terror

Live Through Today

Saddam Hussein is the President for Life of Iraq and author of nine previous self-help books including How to Argue and Win Every Time, The Sanctions Diet, *and* Chicken Soup for the Megalomaniacal Despot's Soul.

ATTENTION DEFICIT DISORDER:

Help Is

They're ADD As Hell,
And They're Not Going To Take It Anymore!

Every day in this country, thousands of people struggle to overcome the stigma and the frustrations of ADD and lead normal – and occasionally extraordinary – lives. Now, in far-ranging interviews, these courageous men and women discuss their personal experiences living with ADD. What they have to say may surprise you:

Fred Mitchem, *Airline Pilot:*
"People said I could never fly a commercial jet because of my condition. What was the question?"

Elaine Wilkinson, *Psychologist:*
"When I was first starting out, my mind used to wander frequently during sessions. I thought I had boring patients, but in fact I was suffering from ADD. Now I focus exclusively on ADD patients, who I see for 3 minutes a session, 15 times a week. It's been a real win-win situation."

Arnold Plotkin, *Founder, ADD Anonymous:*
"ADDA has been immensely liberating. After years of apologizing for my condition, I was at last able to stand before a group of supportive peers and announce, 'Hello. My name is Arnold Plotkin, and I forgot what I was going to say!'"

Alan Kneipf, *MTV Programming Executive:*
"We don't consider ADD an illness. We see it as the choice of a new generation."

Alison Monroe, *Journalist:*
"Surveys show there are many newspaper and TV news reporters suffering from ADD. But they tell only part of the story."

"We all thought it was great!"
– Ellen McGillecuttie, author of
Multiple Personality Disorder:
You Are Not Alone

1099 2579 919

A Totally Random House Publication

REVIVING OPHELIA

THE ROYAL SHAKESPEARE COMPANY'S EMERGENCY PREPAREDNESS HANDBOOK

"All the world's a stage, but some people fall off the stage and dislocate their shoulder; you need to be prepared."

-DAVID BRAUSE, author of *Long Day's Journey Into The Orchestra Pit*

NOW AVAILABLE in audiocassette read by Kenneth Branaugh!

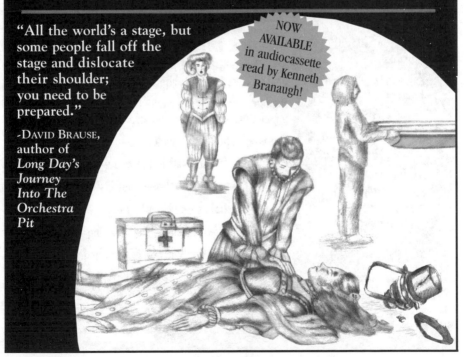

EACH YEAR, ONE OUT OF EVERY TEN SHAKESPEAREAN ACTORS SUSTAINS AN INJURY SERIOUS ENOUGH TO REQUIRE MEDICAL ATTENTION

Beware the ides of March. And April. And October. The truth is, there is no time to let down your guard when it comes to emergency preparedness. Accidents happen, and every time a performer struts and frets his hour upon the stage, he is putting himself at the risk of faulty sets, mishandled props, and simple human error. When the slings and arrows of outrageous fortune befall your Shakespeare production, will you know what to do?

The Royal Shakespeare Company has taken up arms against this sea of troubles with a new comprehensive emergency handbook. Having mounted over 300 productions, they are familiar with all of the injuries one might sustain while putting on the Bard's work, including everything from fog inhalation to codpiece rash to spear wounds. Honored with a special Tony Award for Occupational Safety, *Reviving Ophelia* promises to take the tragedy out of your tragedies, give your comedies some relief, and allow your histories to repeat themselves.

YOU'LL LEARN WHAT TO DO IF:

A wall sconce ignites Julius Caesar's toga seconds before he is to be stabbed.

Romeo's trellis breaks away from the balcony, sending him hurtling into the wings.

The wind machine blows King Lear into the audience.

Prospero pokes himself in the eye with his staff.

The First Gravedigger throws out his back.

Henry VIII chokes on his turkey leg.

Witch #3 scalds herself on the bubbling cauldron.

Bottom gets heat exhaustion inside the donkey head.

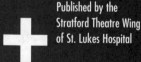

Published by the
Stratford Theatre Wing
of St. Lukes Hospital

$11.95

911 289 102 911

BUNS OF STEEL

AND OTHER PRACTICAL JOKES FOR BAKERS

"A treasure trove of tricky treats!"
Mike Rozen,
Manager,
Hard Roll Cafe

RAMÓN
FRENCH

BAKE YOURSELF SILLY!

$8.99

No one needs to tell you that baking is a stressful job. The constant repetition of egg-beating, dough-kneading and pan-buttering can twist a mentally healthy person into a garlic knot of tension. Combine that with the long hours and sweltering conditions, and it's almost enough to make you boil over!

When you're feeling hot and cross, laughter is a great way to let off steam, and *Buns of Steel* provides you with dozens of zany prank baked goods that are sure to get a rise out of bakers and nonbakers alike. Guaranteed to please your palate as well as your funnybone, these dastardly treats will bring a little emotional leavening into the lives of some very stressed out people – including yourself!

Baguette-Through-The- Head

Exploding Breadstick

Way-Too-Sticky Bun

Whoopee Pita

"After a long holiday weekend, the pigs-in-the-electric-blanket was just what we needed to jolt us back into the work week."

— ANNE BARKIN, BARKIN CATERING

Drawing from the Right Side of the Bong

And Other Tips For First-Time Stoners

Brent "Supertoke" Dillwood
Author of *Weediquette*

$12.99

Don't Be A Mariwannabe!!!

There is nothing more embarrassing than blowing your first high. Whether it be getting the chokes, spilling the bongwater, or just bumming people out with incessant pot-induced babble, you don't want your first date with Mary Jane to be harshed in any way. That's why I created this book, just for you newbies, so that you can partake of the sweet leaf with full confidence and enjoyment, and so that the people you smoke with will invite you back for MORE HERB!!!

Why listen to me? Because I've got mucho experience with the doobage, having toured for 12 years with the Grateful Dead selling pot-filled burritos. I have also been chosen as the Glaucoma Foundation's official liaison, going to afflicted people's homes and teaching them how to roll, smoke and cook with the holy skank.

In the course of my life I have personally turned on over 10,000 people. I want you to be next. All it takes is an open mind and some killer weed.

INCLUDES A GANJA GLOSSARY:

HEMP-MO-TIZED - Feeling zoned out after smoking

BABY FINSTER - Tiny joint

CARPET PATROL - Searching the floor for roaches

JAMES BONG - The most stoned person in the group

LOU WEED - Person who's always got pot

AMISH - Totally wasted

You'll learn many tricks of the bongologist's trade, such as:

- The secret cure for cotton-mouth (Hint: it comes out of the faucet)
- Turning an apple into a waterpipe
- What to do if your hands get really big
- The stoner's emergency kit - papers, twinkies, visine

958 263 11239

Printed On Rolling Paper - **SMOKE THIS BOOK** - Printed On Rolling Paper

GETTING TO

YES

IN AN HOUR OR LESS

Negotiating Tips For
Getting The Love You Want

Wilt Chamberlain

*"Stop tossing up bricks from the three-point line of love!
Getting to Yes tells you everything you need to know to
make your move and go in strong against even the tough-
est defense."* — MIKE LITSKY, author of *The Pickup Game*

NOW SERVING

2 0 0 0

"It's not about 'getting lucky'; it's about hard work and determination. You've got to want it so bad that you're willing to get out there every day and just drill, drill, drill."

— Wilt Chamberlain

EVER SINCE his astonishing admission in his 1992 autobiography,

The View From Above, that he'd had sex with over 20,000 women since the age of 16 — an average of almost two per day — Wilt "The Stilt" Chamberlain has been flooded with requests to reveal his off-court courtship secrets. Now, pro basketball's most venereal player and twelve-time "Nookie of the Year" recipient shares the techniques that have made him America's poster boy for promiscuity.

Inside, you'll study Wilt's patented Fast Break techniques that will take you from "Come here often?" to "Thank you, ma'am" with almost any woman, in under an hour. Wilt covers common objections women raise, from "It's past my curfew" to "I'm here with my husband." He also gives you detailed instructions on how to execute the following basic moves:

➥ BREAK THE DOUBLE TEAM: Getting her away from her unattractive girlfriend.

➥ PICK AND ROLL: Choosing and putting on the right condom.

➥ COME UP WITH THE REBOUND: When she shoots you down in flames.

➥ HEAD FAKE: "Of course I'll respect you. I'll respect you even more..."

➥ GO MAN-TO-MAN: Double your potential sexual partners.

➥ THE "HAIL MARY": Making time with a Catholic girl.

➥ GIVE AND GO: Twenty tried-and-true excuses for making your getaway.

1211 876 9 10998

$ 11.95

BONUS SECTION: Break a "Rules Girl" in just 20 Minutes.

"WHAT THE HELL IS HAPPENING TO ME?"

A Survival Guide
for the
Teenage Werewolf

REAL WEREWOLVES. REAL ISSUES.

"It freaked me out a bit, the first time. One
minute I'm a normal teenager walking home
from school; the next I'm chasing a Buick
down Route 9. It can be hard to adjust."
— Jon Jacobs, Age 13

"I was considered a nerd in high school. The
other kids used to make fun of me, call me
names. Their mistake."
— Ellen Lensen, Age 19

"My schoolwork definitely suffered. I'd show
up for class without my homework, and I'd
have no excuse — I mean, who's going to
believe I ate it?"
— Evan Shweky, Age 17

REAL ANSWERS.

Adolescence is a difficult time for any young person, but it can be par-
ticularly awkward for boys and girls who metamorphose into huge,
bloodthirsty wolves when the moon is full. Teenage werewolves may be
frightened or embarrassed by the changes that take place in their bod-
ies during their monthly cycle: the painful seizures; sudden growth of
hair and fangs; and insatiable appetite for human flesh. *What The Hell Is
Happening To Me?* is a frank yet sympathetic guide that young lycan-
thropes can turn to for support and for practical information on all
aspects of wolfdom during this difficult transitional period.

Also by the Same Authors: *Where the Hell Did I
Come From?* Explains the facts of eternal life to
the newly-resurrected undead.

$9.98

An Algonquin Hound Table Publication

4859 29 193

The One Minuteman Manager

Management Tips from the Revolutionary War

A CLASSIC!
Whether you manage
a home, a business,
or a ragtag band of
revolutionary soldiers...
it works!

Washington Jefferson Smith

Listen my children and you shall hear
The greatest leadership book of the year!

IF your company were threatened by a hostile takeover, could you mobilize your department at a moment's notice?

WHEN was the last time you mustered your salesforce with a fife and drum processional?

HOW many of your downsized employees would proclaim, "I regret that I have but one life to give for my company!"

Utilizing common-sense leadership techniques gleaned from the Revolutionary War, *The One Minuteman Manager* is the breakthrough book that will change the way you think about management forever. These apparently simple methods work just as well with a salesforce today as they did with an infantry back in 1776. Just ask these battle-tested veterans:

"When headquarters raised the prices at the employee cafeteria, I got my entire department to go down there, gather up all the coffee and tea bags and throw them out the window."
— *Leigh Hayden, Hancock Securities*

"We don't have mandatory drug testing at our office, so I usually give people the benefit of the doubt. Even if I'm suspicious, I never fire until I see the whites of their eyes."
— *Richard Winters, Liberty Travel*

"My company's 'No Vacation Without Representation' policy has cut our sick days in half."
— *Peter Tuneski, U.S. Pewter*

$17.76

ON
DEATH
AND
DINING

How To Make Your Last Meal "To Die For"

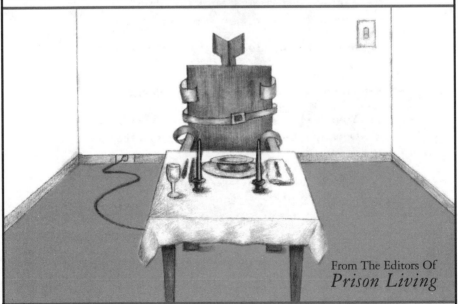

From The Editors Of
Prison Living

"Do not go hungry into that good night. Read this book!"
– THE GALLOWING GOURMET

Fed Man Walking!

When you're dining in the valley of the shadow of death, you want to make your last meal something special. This delightful volume is filled with hundreds of sumptuous suggestions created specifically for the death row inmate. Whether you choose sit-down or buffet, meat or vegetarian, haute cuisine or diner fare, we'll provide you with the makings for an unforgettable last meal. It's the perfect way to say "Goodbye, gruel world!"

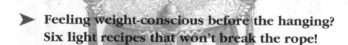

➤ **Feeling weight-conscious before the hanging? Six light recipes that won't break the rope!**

➤ **Zesty Entrees – 500-volt Chili, Firing Squab, Satay of Execution, and others.**

➤ **Famous Last Meals – Eggs Goebbels, Chicken Gilmore, Lobster Bundy.**

➤ **Religious Dilemma – Is this the time to try the pork?**

➤ **The perfect wine for a lethal injection.**

➤ **Your Just Desserts – Death by Chocolate, Decappucino, and other sweet rewards.**

➤ **Go out with a bang! Swallow raw popping corn before the electrocution.**

...and much more!!

"Don't think of it as your last meal; think of it as the first meal of the rest of your life, which just happens to end tomorrow at 6 a.m."

— HERB EMANUELSON, WARDEN, SING-SING

FINAL EXIT STAGE LEFT

When An Actor You Love Needs Career Termination

MARYANNE PISCIPO

What do these actors and many more have in common?

They are all suffering from painful and degenerative acting careers. Intellectually, they know that their fifteen minutes are up, and that things probably won't get any better. Yet they press on, taking jobs that compromise what little artistic dignity they have left.

Until recently, this behavior pattern had not been recognized or treated, but finally there is a compassionate solution. ACT (Assisted Career Termination) is a program of intervention designed to gradually wean the actor off of his or her ailing career as humanely as possible. It was created for the actor's family, agent, manager, and friends – the people who care most and the people who must ultimately decide on the sensitive issue of career termination.

How do you know if an actor you love is suffering from a terminally ailing career? Look for these danger signs:

- Dinner Theater in Ottowa
- Skin Care Infomercials
- Books on Tape
- Celebrity Golf Tournaments
- Any Production of a Neil Simon Play
- TV Cast Reunion Specials
- Corporate Training Films
- A Guest Appearance on *Murder, She Wrote*
- Dubbing Asian Horror Films
- Celebrity Judge in Local Talent Show

"The book has been my rock during this very difficult time. Loni is beginning to see the light, and I think we're going to make it."
— Name Withheld Upon Request

3948 485 2191

Suggestions
for
Further Reading

(As if you haven't read enough already...)

Awaken the Giant Within Your Shorts

Awaken the Giant Bug Within: Kafka's Guide to Personal Transformation

Smart Women, Silly Rabbit

10 Stupid Things Women Do to Mess Up Their Livestock

Prozac United Nations

The Courage to Heel

Listening to Balzac

The 7 Habits of Highly Infectious People

The 7 Habits of Highly Reflective Nuns

The 7 Habitrails of Highly Affectionate Gerbils

The 7 Digits of Highly Effective Phone Numbers

The 7 Abbots of Highly Effective Costellos

The 7 Rabbits of Highly Effective Magicians

Martha Stewart Prison Living

Chicken Soup for Soul Asylum

The Autist's Way

Emotional Intelligence: The Unheralded Branch of the CIA

The Cellophane Prophesy

What to Expect When You're Expectorating

What to Expect When You're Prospecting

What to Expect When You're Disrespecting:
A Smack!

Do What You Love and the Monkey Will Follow

Nasal Passages

Wimple Abundance

The Drachma of the Gifted Child

The Grandma of the Gifted Child

Finding Flo'

The Wart of R.

The Tao of Zen

The Pooh of Mao

The Taco of Poo

You Just Don't Understand: Women and Ducks
in Conversation

Goo Sex With Dr. Ruth Westheimer

The Course in Mackerels

Carp of the Soul

The Soul's Cod

The One Minute Manger

Don't Sweat In the Chicken Soup

Simplify Your Afterlife

The Complete Idiot's Guide to Experimental Neurosurgery

Rocket Science for Dummies

Banjo for Sluts

Life's Little Liposuction Book

Life's Little Resurrection Book

Life's Little Deduction Book

Life's Little Dissection Book

14,000 Thongs to Be Happy About

14,000 Things to Be Happy Beneath

14,000 Things to Be Happy Despite

14,000 Things to Be Slap Happy About

14,000 Things in My Basement

MMMMMMMMMMMMMM Things for Ancient Romans to Be Happy About

6.02252 X 10^23 Things for Avogadro to Be Happy About

12, 24, or 36 Things for Photographers to Be Happy About

50 (+/- 15) Things for Social Scientists to Be Happy About

1 Thing for Buddha to Be Happy About

Billions and Billions of Things for Carl Sagan to Be Happy About

Buns of Steely Dan

Women Who Run With Wolf Blitzer

Women Who Run From the Police

Inert Tennis

A Gathering of Mennonites

How to Win Franz and Influence Dieter: Negotiating With Germans

Life 101010101: The Computer Programmer's Guide to Life

Life 201: A Guide to Living in New Jersey

Looking Out for #2

The Cinderfella Complex

Never Let Them See You Sweat the Small Stuff

Spontaneous Kneeling

Spontaneous Whaling

Twit for Life

Thin Ties in Thirty Days

The Joy of Phone Sex

The Joy of Sikhs

The Goy of Sex

My Mother, My Serf

Our Booties, Ourselves

Our Bradies, Ourselves

Think and Grow, Bitch!

Eat Bait, Lose Weight

It's Not Who You're Eating, It's Who's Eating You

The Tibetan Book of the Injured

The Tibetan Book of the Grateful Dead

Dr. Atkins Nude Diet Revolution

Pulling Your Own Hamstrings

I'm DOA, You're DOA

I'm OK...Right?

Cross-Dress for Success

Hooked on Ebonics

Mars and Venus on a Bender

All I Know I Learned at a Gathering of Men Who Hate Women and Influence People and the Women Who Love Them Too Much

Photo/Art Credits:

The Authors

Jonathan Bines is a regular contributor of humor to local and national publications, and is head writer of the sketch comedy group, The Associates. The author of the humor book *Bushisms*, he has worked on the editorial staff of *Harper's Magazine* and *The New Republic*, and is currently a columnist for *New York Press*. He performs stand-up and sketch comedy at clubs in New York City.

Gary Greenberg is a nationally-touring stand-up comedian and writer based in Manhattan. He has written segments for Comedy Central's *The Daily Show* and The USA Network's "Up All Night." Selected by The Toyota Comedy Festival as one of New York's top clean comics, he is a featured performer at clubs and colleges across the country.